7 REASONS
LIFE IS BETTER
WITH
GOD

NATHAN BROWN

Autumn
House® Publishing
www.autumnhousepublishing.com
A Division of **REVIEW AND HERALD® PUBLISHING**
Since 1861

The author assumes full responsibility for the accuracy of all facts and quotations as cited in this book.

Unless otherwise indicated, all Scripture quotations are taken from the *Holy Bible,* New Living Translation, copyright © 1996. Used by permission of Tyndale House Publishers, Inc., Wheaton, Illinois 60189. All rights reserved.

Texts credited to Message are from *The Message.* Copyright © 1993, 1994, 1995, 1996, 2000, 2001, 2002. Used by permission of NavPress Publishing Group.
Texts credited to NIV are from the *Holy Bible, New International Version.* Copyright © 1973, 1978, 1984, International Bible Society. Used by permission of Zondervan Bible Publishers.
Verses marked TLB are taken from *The Living Bible,* copyright © 1971 by Tyndale House Publishers, Wheaton, Ill. Used by permission.

This book was
Edited by Gerald Wheeler
Copyedited by Delma Miller and James Cavil
Cover design by Trent Truman
Interior design by Candy Harvey
Electronic makeup by Shirley M. Bolivar
Typeset: 12/14.5 Bembo

PRINTED IN U.S.A.

11 10 09 08 07   5 4 3 2 1

Library of Congress Cataloging-in-Publication Data
Brown, Nathan, 1974-   .
    7 reasons life is better with God/Nathan Brown.
        p. cm.
    ISBN 978-0-8127-0436-5
    1. Spirituality. 2. Christian life. 3. Apologetics. I. Title. II. Title: Seven reasons life is better with God.
    BV4501.3.B772 2006
    248.4—dc22

                                        2006035014

DEDICATED TO

my wife, my parents,
and all other people
who have helped me appreciate something more
of the reasons that life is better with God.

ACKNOWLEDGMENTS

Portions of this book have appeared in slightly different form in *Adventist Review, Record, Insight, Signs of the Times* (Australia), *Signs of the Times* (U.S.A.), *Message, The Edge, CQ,* and *Real-Time Faith.*

CONTENTS

INTRODUCTION:
WHY LIFE IS BETTER WITH GOD

For many people in the Western world life seems as good as it gets. For the most part, we're well fed, well educated, and well-off. We are most concerned not about finding opportunities but how to choose the most satisfying options out of a whole range of possibilities. P. J. O'Rourke in his *All the Trouble in the World* concludes that—from many perspectives—things have never been better, and if anyone wants to argue against that he just needs to say one word: "Dentistry!" In many ways we are so devoid of real problems that we spend hours borrowing those of other people through television news and dramas.

So why do we need God? When we seem to have all our basic needs covered, why complicate our lives with Something or Someone so strange and different? Isn't religion just what old, poor, and sick people use to feel better about themselves? Isn't church just a bunch of hypocrites—or, at best, people like you and me? Sure, we all have disappointments, but when things are going pretty well, tell me then why the God/faith/religion/church thing matters.

The next few pages are an attempt to answer some aspects of these questions. I believe the God/faith/religion/church thing does matter. A lot. Whether you're on top of the world with more opportunities than you could ever imagine or living on the streets with no money, no family, and no hope, God matters just the same. Here are seven reasons that life is simply better with Him:

Because God is and not because of who you are. Whatever we may think of Him makes little difference to the reality of His existence and His nature.

Because life is great. Life has some things so wonderful that we need to thank Someone for them. The best in life is better still when we recognize a bigger source and purpose behind it.

Because life hurts. Sometimes—perhaps far too often—life is not so great. God does not necessarily answer all the questions about why things happen to ruin it, but He does give direction, strength, and hope that will enable us to cope with them.

Because you can make a difference. Life isn't just about us. The privilege of helping others and representing God to them is another facet of life lived at its best.

Because life ends. Death is something that we cannot avoid. We can deny it, but we cannot escape its effects on our families, our friends, and ultimately ourselves. A funeral is one of those occasions that raise the big questions in life and prompt us back to the big answers.

Because life begins again. What if this life is not all there is meant to be? When our choices have impacts that can last forever, suddenly our decisions are infinitely important.

Because God loves each of us. This is His nature. If God did not love us, He would not be God. Whether we accept or reject His love, that love must have an impact on our existence.

This book explores these reasons from a number of angles. We think in different ways, and so we could each explain them in countless ways. Hopefully, this book will prompt you to come up with your own reasons that the God/faith/religion/church thing matters, and that life is better with God. But feel free to keep some of these perspectives as well.

One way or another, the God/faith/religion/church thing is vital. When we realize that life is better with God, we will recognize that our response to Him will make all the difference both to us and to those around us.

Because God Is

God Exists

In *One Hundred Years of Solitude* Gabriel Garcia Marquez tells the story of a plague of forgetting that swept through the village in which the novel takes place. Faced with losing their memory and thus all their knowledge, the townspeople decided to label everything around them to preserve their memories for as long as possible. They named their household items: table, chair, clock, door, and bed. Then they turned their attention to the animals and plants: cow, goat, pig, hen, cassava, and banana.

However, as the disease progressed, they became concerned that, while they might be able to recognize the objects from the labels, they might not be able to recall their use. So the labels became more complex, detailing how they regularly employed the objects, plants, and animals. The people got together to erect signs of significance to the whole village. The one dominating the main street declared: "GOD EXISTS." It was the one thing they all needed to remember no matter how much else they forgot.

In the face of life's many uncertainties and our own forgetfulness, the truth of God's existence is something we should always strive to keep in mind. Our only hope lies in His existence and His goodness. If either of those elements vanishes, then we are lost.

That is the significance of God's statement to Moses from the burning bush. In the midst of the ongoing slavery of God's people and Moses' personal confusion, the Lord announced Himself in the terms they most needed to hear: "I AM" (Ex. 3:14).

Centuries later Jesus employed the same phrase to declare to the people of His day who He was: "I tell you the truth, . . . before Abraham was born, I am!" (John 8:58, NIV). His listeners did not miss what He was getting at—in fact, it so incensed some of them that they tried to stone Him.

The affirmation of God's eternal existence is also a part of the praise before God's throne described in Revelation. The four living creatures continually proclaim Him as He "who was, and is, and is to come" (Rev. 4:8, NIV).

It is the biggest claim that it is possible to make—and throughout the Bible God continually applies it to Himself. "I AM" describes both His eternal present and His eternal presence.

Scripture portrays God in many ways. It tells how His overwhelming greatness and power is praised forever. However, one of the most mentioned divine attributes is His love. Psalm 136 is a high point of God's love. The writer lists point after point—from the natural world, from history, and from God's dealings with His people individually—and repeatedly refers the reader back to the love of God: "His love endures forever" (NIV). Even God's greatness we find ultimately attributed to His great and endless love.

However, as we read through the whole book of Psalms, we discover that the concept is not just a nice refrain to create a poetic effect in one psalm. The assertion appears in psalm after psalm: "His love endures forever."

"God is love" is certainly true. However, it might be more correct to say—in the same way as we do that "God is"—"God's love is."

With the assurance of such an eternal love, our personal circumstances become less important, because, even if we lose everything, God's love remains and—as Paul put it—nothing can sever us from that love: "neither death nor life, neither angels nor demons, neither the present nor the future, nor any powers, neither height nor depth, nor anything else in all creation, will be able to separate us from the love of God that is in Christ Jesus our Lord" (Rom. 8:38, 39, NIV). Put simply, in Jesus and His death for us we have conclusive and enduring proof of both God's existence and His love.

The whole thing is hugely mind-boggling. Yet we continually find ourselves fighting a plague of forgetting. And even if we do not forget the theory, we too easily forget it in practice. Maybe we need to put up signs to remind us. Perhaps you need to photocopy it several times, then stick it on the mirror or the fridge or the steering wheel.

God exists. God is. God's love is. And if you are not sure of that fact, look at the cross. The sacrifice of the Son of God says it all.

The Big Bet?

In Pascal's *Pensées* the seventeenth-century French mathematician and philosopher proposed a suitably mathematical approach to faith. In a formulation that has come to be known as Pascal's wager he suggests we can look at the truth of the God of Christianity as a game of chance.

When it comes down to it, he argues, "either God is or He is not." The difficulty is that reason alone cannot get us beyond this point. We cannot argue conclusively either His existence or nonexistence. However, Pascal maintains it is an unavoidable choice—it is simply a matter of which way to choose. Because of its inevitability, "your reason is no more affronted by choosing one rather than the other," he writes—both are equally legitimate options.

Pascal's solution is to look at what is to be won and lost in the cosmic wager he proposes: "If you win you win everything, if you lose you lose nothing." In other words, if God exists as we believe, we receive eternal life and all the promises of the Bible, and if He does not exist, we die. While that is the end of the story for us, it is what would have happened anyway. According to Pascal, while the odds of God existing may be only one in an infinite number of possibilities, we risk nothing by betting that way—and have everything to gain.

Christians have adopted and repeated the argument in a variety of forms since he first published *Pensées* in the 1660s. But the question remains whether his wager constitutes sufficient justification of and foundation for a credible belief in God. Doubt still nags us. As William James, an American philosopher writing in the 1890s, suggested, "you probably feel that when religious faith expresses itself thus, in the language of the gaming table, it is put to its last trumps" *(The Will to Believe).*

It seems that even Paul, writing in the New Testament, was uncomfortable with arguments along the lines of Pascal's. "If Christ has not been raised [the central tenet of Christian faith], our preaching is useless and so is your faith. . . . If only for this life we have hope in Christ, we are to be pitied more than all men" (1 Cor. 15:14-19, NIV). For Paul, it is not good enough to conclude that if it is not true, we have not lost anything. The truth or otherwise of God and the claims of Christianity are of utmost importance.

Another problem James identifies in Pascal's proposition is that we can equally apply it to any other formulation of belief—Hindu, Buddhist, Muslim, or whatever promise of eternal reward. Thus it can only be a clinching argument for a Christian God when the prospective believer has a preexisting tendency toward such a belief.

So we find ourselves back at the uncertain position in which we began, unable to argue our way forward. However, it does not have to be the end of our search for God or faith. "In truths dependent on our personal action, then, faith based on desire is certainly a lawful and possibly an indispensable thing" (James, *The Will to Believe*). Thankfully, the possibility of faith in God does not depend upon our ability to argue philosophy.

James argues for a freedom to choose: "a rule of thinking which would absolutely prevent me from acknowledging certain kinds of truth if those kinds of truth were really there would be an irrational rule" *(ibid.).* In addition, it is not irrational to believe in that for which rationality can provide no answers. Even then, we find evidence of God in our lives, in the world around us, and in history— "too much to deny and too little to be sure" (Pascal)—and it is always a matter of choice. But we respond not as a gambler but as a pilgrim on a journey toward truth.

So Far Away, So Close

"You . . . You whom we love . . . You cannot see us. You cannot hear us. You imagine us so far away, and yet we are so close" (the opening lines of *Faraway, So Close!* a 1993 film by Wim Wenders).

In the opening scene of the movie the angel looking across the city awakes echoes of Jesus lamenting over Jerusalem. As the angel surveys the traffic and people going about their everyday business, he realizes that they cannot imagine God and His angels playing any real role in their lives. God is a deity of distance—far removed from what they regard as the real world around them. The thoughts expressed by the angel identify our greatest difficulties in gaining a concept of God. We imagine Him far away when yet He is so close.

Our first difficulty is in imagining a God big enough. We try to place Him in a box shaped of our own ideas. "We degrade Providence too much by attributing our ideas to it out of annoyance at being unable to understand it" (Dostoyevsky, *The Idiot*). But we can begin to overcome this by sensing our own smallness in a vast universe. Even our own insignificance in relation to our world as a whole can teach us something vital. We can begin to recognize that a power so great as to create and sustain a vast array of galaxies and worlds is definitely worthy of our respect, our worship, and our obedience. However, this is still a distant God, one difficult to love. Most often we will fear such a deity.

This leads to the second and greater difficulty. As human beings we need a God small enough for us to hug, because that is the way we love. We must have a deity compact enough to care for our microscopic beings, thus a close God. C. S. Lewis suggests that God is so large as to be able to fit the whole of the universe inside Himself without being stretched but also so small as to be able to fit inside the tiniest flower seed without being compressed. In this paradox lies the true greatness of God and His dealings with our world.

"'God is great' . . . is a truth which needed no supernatural being to teach men. That God is little, that is the truth which Jesus taught man" (Father Neville Figgis, as quoted by Philip Yancey in *The Jesus I Never Knew*). In Jesus we have the human face of God. God set up a branch office in our little corner of the universe. It is this Deity that we can love and that we can serve properly. Such a God can feel our pain, our sorrow, our frustration, our joy, and our hopes.

Too often we accept a faraway God without appreciating His actual nearness. We acknowledge the Almighty and a future with God but fail to recognize the God who dwelt among us and who is our present friend. While the hope of final deliverance is real and we should never undervalue it, it is only God's sacrificial stoop to our level, His identification with us and His sympathy with our predicament, that makes such hope hopeful.

Yes, we can rejoice in the incredible greatness of God, but without a small God, a huge God is truly terrifying. It is only through appreciation of the littleness of God that the even more incredible greatness of God is revealed. This is a God whom we can worship and love and who truly loves us. It is a God who is more real than everything that we can see around us. Such a God can and wants to be a part of our lives.

Here we have the divine glorious paradox: He is both the ultimate and all-powerful ruler of the universe and our personal friend. Only our response to Him determines our distance from God, and even then we will always find Him if we just turn and look for Him. In His greatness God is further from us than we can possibly imagine, and yet He wants to be our closest friend. He is far away and yet so near.

Jesus + Nothing

Here is something I do not often get to admit in public: I was captain of my high school's mathematics team. No, I am not ashamed of it—it just never seems to come up in conversation. After all, it is not like being in the starting five of the school basketball team or acting a major role in the school play or musical.

I guess it is hardly unusual that it is not a common topic of conversation, because I am sure most people in my school would have been surprised to know we even had a math team. But it is a true story.

A friend and I signed up—I think the opportunity may have involved a couple days off from school—and, to our amazement, we had fun. Equally surprisingly, we were only narrowly defeated in the regional final. It could be the raw material for another story idea on the agony of missed opportunity. However, such a defeat will undoubtedly fail to arouse any great sympathy, given the general ambivalence afforded mathematics tournaments.

Of course, the fun we had was largely of our own creation—mathematics should be a serious business—and one of the foremost avenues of our humor was the discovery of the power of the formula. A significant part of our "training" focused on learning and applying formulas appropriate to a given problem. As anyone who has done a high school math exam will know, usually at least half of the points for any question involve the process whereby the problem is worked through, regardless of the correctness or otherwise of the answer. The right formula is an important step in the problem-solving process. Applying it is the surest way to get to the correct answer—even if it might not have worked out in that particular instance. When the student can recognize when to use that formula, they will be more likely to arrive at the answer more often.

However, we took the idea of the formula and began to apply it beyond the world of mathematics. We interchanged words, phrases, and meanings to prove whatever we wanted to. Sometimes we used this process to arrive at a predetermined conclusion, or we would start with a single statement and substitute the various components and see where our illogical logic took us. I think we used the concept of the formula to complicate simple things—and provide ourselves with some mostly harmless entertainment. However, the true use of a formula is to capture the essence of a process whereby we can solve a problem or determine a value.

I was reminded of this way of approaching life when I particularly noticed a line from a song at a concert. It had a simple but all-encompassing formula: "Jesus plus nothing equals everything."

Scientists have long been working to develop a theory to explain the whole universe. However, in Jesus we have it. Through Him all things came into being, and He continues to give life and light (John 1:1-5). It is the formula of everything.

As such, it is an all-encompassing truth. It often takes the form of a question. Psalm 73 asks: "Whom have I in heaven but you? I desire you more than anything on earth" (verse 25).

Peter echoed this sentiment when challenged by Jesus Himself. Christ asked the disciples if they wanted to leave Him. Peter immediately replied, "Lord, to whom would we go?" (John 6:68).

His own experience made Paul equally definite. He writes: "Everything else is worthless when compared with the priceless gain of knowing Christ Jesus my Lord. I have discarded everything else, counting it all as garbage, so that I may have Christ and become one with him. I no longer count on my own goodness or my ability to obey God's law, but I trust Christ to save me" (Phil. 3:8, 9).

It's a simple formula. Nothing can add to Jesus—and equally certain, you can do nothing to add to Jesus and what He has done for you. If you have Jesus, you have everything. But if you do not have Him, then you have nothing.

The Disappointment of the Resurrection

E aster Saturday must have been one of the strangest days in history. The whole universe must have held its breath waiting for the next day, wondering whether the promised resurrection was possible or whether God's plan might have come to an unfortunate end.

The disciples, who had far less of an idea as to what was actually going on, huddled together behind a locked door. The emotions they were all battling were incredible. First, they struggled with heartbroken grief. Jesus had been their friend and their teacher. After a couple years traveling around the countryside with Him, their simple friendship was strong. Now He was dead.

The disciples also had dared to believe that Jesus was the Messiah for whom their people had been waiting. Now that seemed to be all gone. Merely a week previously Jesus had seemed to begin what they thought would be the exercise of His Messiahship as the crowd acclaimed Him during His triumphal entry into Jerusalem. Now He was dead after enduring great agony and shame. It was not quite the fate anyone expected of the Messiah.

The disciples were scared. They feared that, as Jesus' closest supporters, they might suffer a similar fate. Since they had all been involved publicly in Jesus' life and ministry, it would have appeared quite possible that the Jewish and Roman leaders would want to clean up the last of a potential uprising by executing the closest of Jesus' followers (John 20:19).

Somewhere in this wave of grief, doubt, and fear, lurking in the back of the disciples' minds, may have been still another emotion. None of them would have wanted to admit the feeling (they would have felt a little guilty about harboring such thoughts), but it was still there and real. It is possible that there might have been just a little relief mixed in with the other emotions that the disciples shared on Easter Saturday.

Jesus had had some strange ideas that the disciples had not properly understood, ones that He often used to disturb their thinking. In addition, He had often done things that did not make sense to them. Now, though, once the Jewish leaders' initial excitement had calmed down, the disciples might have imagined that they would be able to return to their fishing and other occupations and live a normal life.

If they could just stay hidden for a few weeks, they could carefully slip back to Galilee, and things could just go on as before. Some of their neighbors might ridicule them for wasting those few years, but that too would settle down in time. They could remember Jesus merely as a great friend and a short-lived hope that they had once had. In a few years they might even be able to share fond memories of their days with their traveling preacher-friend.

Instead, their emotional maelstrom intensified after the women visited Jesus' grave early on the morning of Easter Sunday. The accounts of their experiences there disturbed the disciples. Later that day Jesus appeared to the two travelers on the road to Emmaus, and they quickly shared their excited story with the confused disciples. Then, suddenly, Jesus appeared among them—real and alive.

On Easter Sunday the disciples had had their emotions shattered once again. It may be that they had retained their hopes for a return to normal life even after they had heard from the women who had brought back the report of the empty tomb. The two disciples had simply headed back home down the road to Emmaus and possibly their homes and jobs. Their disappointment was obvious from their conversation, but they were nevertheless returning home after

23

Passover weekend. But Jesus had turned them around, and any hope of a normal life was out of the question (Luke 24:13–35).

Now all the disciples struggled to come to terms with the reality of the resurrected Christ. Seven of them, at Peter's suggestion, did briefly attempt to resume their former life as fishermen, but again Jesus interrupted their halfhearted attempt at normality (John 21). Mingled with the joy that Peter felt that morning on the beach must have been some trepidation about his denial just prior to the Crucifixion. But Jesus took special care to allay his fear.

As they spent time with Jesus during the six weeks following the Resurrection, the disciples' grief and fear evaporated, but their sense of relief also vanished. Somewhere in the darkest corners of their hearts may have lurked just a tinge of disappointment. When they were faced with the glorious certainty of the resurrected Messiah, such disappointment would have quickly faded into insignificance, but it may well have continued to be part of the emotional turmoil they had to deal with. That was why Jesus took time to explain His death and resurrection on the road to Emmaus; He answered the specific doubts of Mary, Thomas, and Peter; and He responded to many of the unspoken fears and questions that pressed upon the disciples.

As a result they found themselves both with no space to doubt and no other options. Jesus now had even larger claims, and they had to do something about them. As He talked with them, the disciples found themselves compelled to believe. At the same time, their responsibilities became clear. Their hope of a return to normalcy transformed into a determination to change the entire world with the message of Jesus as the Christ. Instead of a retreat from the things they had halfheartedly believed prior to the Crucifixion, they now embraced them more fully and truly.

As Christians, "in a real sense we live on Saturday, the day with no name" (Philip Yancey, *The Jesus I Never Knew*). Because we live in a world in which God too often seems remote, it is easy to feel that He is of little consequence to our everyday lives. We can live with God a long way off, as if it is Easter Saturday. Yes, we may have known Him, but hopefully He might not bother us anymore. At times, we might feel some distress at our distance from God, but there is also some sense of relief.

Milan Kundera suggests that "the Christian believes in God in the full certainty that He will remain invisible" and that there is a certain "kind of terror a Christian might feel on receiving a telephone call from God, announcing that He was coming over for dinner" *(The Farewell Party)*. As humans, we think we are most happy when left to ourselves. Except in our most desperate circumstances, we find a respectful distance between God and us comforting.

But there always comes a point at which Jesus must become alive and real to us. This can involve a process of working through the realities behind the claims Jesus made. Or it can be something akin to the disciples' experience during the weeks following Easter Sunday. While we might be searching for hope, the kind that Jesus presents us often does not match our expectations, and we may endure disappointment.

However, when Jesus does become real to us, it summons us to live differently. God calls us to live beyond ourselves in the certainty of Jesus' death, resurrection, and love for us. The reality of Christ's resurrection in our lives must make a difference. "The disciples who lived through both days, Friday and Sunday, never doubted God again" (Yancey, *The Jesus I Never Knew*). The change that the Lord worked in the lives of the 11 disciples confirms the glorious truth of the Resurrection. It is such a transformation that must reshape our own lives.

As one writer put it: "True Christianity calls us to live on a cold and windy mountaintop, not on the flattened plain of reasonable, middle-of-the-road religion." The only way in which we can overcome the inevitable disappointment of the resurrection of Christ is to view it in the light of God's great love. We must cling to that which causes the most discomfort to us as sinful people. Only then will we find Christ's resurrection to be the source of ultimate comfort and hope and be able to truly rejoice in the triumph of the Resurrection on that Sunday morning.

A Vision of God

Outside the small town of Tennant Creek, in the middle of the Northern Territory—the Australian out-back—there exists a huge hole in the ground. It is all that remains of the open-cut Nobles Nob gold mine. For many years, starting in the 1930s, it was Australia's richest gold mine. But other mining companies elsewhere across Australia left similar holes, so that fact is hardly notable.

However, what is remarkable is the story of the people who found this rich deposit of gold and staked the original claim. "It is said that the find was made by the unlikely partnership of a one-eyed man called John Noble and the blind William Weaber" *(Australian Motoring Guide).* One's first reaction when surveying the harsh countryside surrounding the abandoned mine is to question why these two men—with one good eye between them—would bother to scratch around in this inhospitable and vast spinifex-infested desert.

Whatever their motivation might have been and however much we might call their sanity into question, we cannot dispute the fact of the discovery. They would not have found the gold deposit if they had simply remained at home. We must admire their commitment to their quest for undiscovered gold. To Jeremiah, God suggests that we should employ a similar level of determination in our search for Him: "If you look for me in earnest, you will find me when you seek me" (Jer. 29:13; cf. Deut. 4:29).

It is even possible that the process of searching with all our heart is more important than the finding. The process of seeking—in line with similar biblical reasoning, such as losing our lives to gain them and taking up the heavy weight of the cross to be relieved of our burdens—may actually be the finding itself, especially when we consider that the Bible states that God is not hiding but is already out looking for us (Luke 15:4).

Whatever else our search involves, God's request for us to look for Him includes a promise that it will be successful. The Bible contains numerous stories of people in pursuit of God in different ways: "Eagerly they sought after God, and they found him" (2 Chron. 15:15). But they did not always encounter Him in the places in which they expected, but when they placed their trust in God's love and goodness, they did discover what they needed.

Ultimately, our search for a vision of God finds its goal in Jesus and His death for us on the cross. This incredible revelation of God was a visible demonstration of who He is and what He is like. Jesus Himself said, "If you had known who I am, then you would have known who my Father is. . . . Anyone who has seen me has seen the Father!" (John 14:7-9). Too often the dust of history may obscure this glimpse of divinity, but it is still a glorious reality: Jesus was "God with us." In getting to know Christ, as depicted in the Gospels, we can see God and how He really loves us.

Although we continue to struggle with imperfect, sin-damaged eyesight as we seek a vision of our God, we do have a promise that one day we will see so much more. Some years after his blinding vision, Paul wrote, "Now we see things imperfectly as in a poor mirror, but then we will see everything with perfect clarity. All that I know now is partial and incomplete, but then I will know everything completely, just as God knows me now" (1 Cor. 13:12). No matter how dark our lives may seem, we can always have something of a "virtual vision" when we rely upon God's promises that one day we will actually see Him face to face. Even if we have no apparent vision, we always have the promise of the complete vision. And—as demonstrated by the unlikely Tennant Creek prospectors—even the blind can find gold when they get out there and start looking.

Taking It Seriously

Writer Annie Dillard asks the question: "Why do we people in churches seem like cheerful, brainless tourists on a packaged tour of the Absolute?" She goes on to observe, "On the whole, I do not find Christians . . . sufficiently sensible of the conditions. Does anyone have the foggiest idea what sort of power we so blithely invoke? Or, as I suspect, does no one believe a word of it? The churches are children playing on the floor with their chemistry sets, mixing up a batch of TNT. . . . It is madness to wear ladies' straw hats and velvet hats to church; we should all be wearing crash helmets. Ushers should issue life preservers and signal flares; they should lash us to our pews" *(Teaching a Stone to Talk: Expeditions and Encounters)*.

It's worth thinking about. Amid the bustle of Sabbath mornings, the mechanics of church organization, and the comfortable mediocrity of our week-to-week religiosity, how often do we stop to think about the "consuming fire" (Heb. 12:29; see also Deut. 4:24), supposedly the center of our faith and lives?

Sometimes God scares me—and He should probably frighten me more often. We need to remember the truism that He is God, and we are not. For our own sakes we must take it seriously. Constantly we talk about friendship with God—and it is an important way of understanding our relationship with our Creator and Savior. But as with all real relationships, we must base it on serious respect. "Friendship with the Lord is reserved for those who fear him" (Ps. 25:14).

We cannot allow God's mystery and magnitude to slip down the back of our religious couches as we settle in for another episode of consumer church.

When we take them seriously, the Bible stories are not just morality tales for children. The same God has touched our own lives, and He is at work in awesome ways. Once we begin to see religion in this way, the death and resurrection of God become the most profound facts of both history *and* the individual stories of our own lives. But without sanctified seriousness, worship will simply be a routine to be endured or a succession of experiences to be sampled. Unless we take it seriously, concern—and action—for the well-being of others will seem merely an optional extra to our convenience Christianity. And until we take it seriously, we will regard the Second Coming as just a nice idea instead of an earthshaking reality—an alternately terrifying threat and a joyful promise.

Only when we take it seriously will the teachings of Jesus begin to make sense in our lives. Not until then can we begin to love our enemies and pray for those who persecute us (see Matt. 5:44), even if it means that we let others rip us off. Taking it seriously enables us to grasp that "treasures in heaven" (see Matt. 6:20) actually do have real value. Until we take it seriously, the Beatitudes (see Matt. 5:2-12) will never sound like more than an exercise in pious idealism. And so on.

Halfhearted faith is nonsense. But then halfhearted unfaith is equally so. Given a glimpse of the eternal significance of our lives, we step back into the banality of our world either with a divine mission or with utter hopelessness. They are the only two options open to us.

But this "taking it seriously" is not a prescription for somber and narrow introspection. Paradoxically, it is the foundation for true joy and creativity. It was precisely because he did take it seriously that Paul could exhort his readers from his prison cell to live lives of rejoicing (see Phil. 4:4). And it is in standing on this solid foundation that we can best celebrate the good things of life, engage with those around us, and risk ourselves for the sake of the kingdom of God.

Perhaps it might be worth dressing differently for church next week—helmets and life preservers recommended—to remind ourselves of the awesome Mystery we approach in worship, in whose terrifying presence we live out our unwitting lives and who reaches down to touch them in alarming, glorious, and eternal ways.

Because Life
Is Great

Anti-Paranoia

Fear has become a fundamental aspect of our culture. If we don't get enough of a thrill from the risks of our everyday lives, we can borrow fear from the popular media as it reports the misfortunes of others and glamorizes them as entertainment. It's easy to believe Kalle Lasn's suggestion that "the first agenda of the commercial media is to sell fear." It's a simple formula: "Fear breeds insecurity—and then consumer culture offers us a variety of ways to buy our way back to security" *(Culture Jam)*.

We could dismiss such a critique as conspiracy paranoia. Indeed, conspiracy theories do abound. It seems almost all of us have a pet theory about how some organization, government, corporation, or individual is working insidiously behind the scenes to bring an end to civilization as we know it. We can find ourselves tempted to search for the sinister shadow behind even the most innocuous event or headline. And of course—as the saying goes—the complete lack of evidence is the ultimate proof the conspiracy is working.

In *The Man Who Was Thursday* G. K. Chesterton tells the story of a young man recruited by a police force to protect the world from an anarchist terrorist plot. Through the twists of the story, Thursday—together with the readers—slowly uncovers a great conspiracy. However, to his great surprise, he discovers an overarching conspiracy of goodness rather than one that sought to destroy. Commenting on his story, Chesterton wrote, "It was intended to describe the world of wild despair and doubt which the pessimists were generally describing, with just a gleam of hope in some double meaning of the doubt, which even the pessimists felt in some fitful fashion" (*Illustrated London News,* June 13, 1936).

To find a double meaning in the doubt and paranoia around us is a most liberating way of looking at the world. Yes, there is a great conspiracy afoot, but—to borrow a line from Amnesty International—it's one of hope. Jesus' repeated announcement throughout His teaching was that the kingdom of God is here and now, even when as small and seemingly insignificant as a mustard seed (Matt. 13:31). Even if it doesn't seem like it, God is working out His purposes in our world: it is a kind of anti-paranoia.

Anti-paranoia will change the way we see the world—and will transform the world itself as a result. Beginning to be a little less skeptical of those around us, we search for the best in whatever we are doing. Our security is not something that can be bought and sold—it rests on a deep-seated suspicion that Something or Someone creates the glimpses of goodness we just cannot ignore. God went to great lengths to reorder our world—He sent His Son to die and to save (John 3:16, 17)—and He is constantly at work in our world and our lives, trying to connect us back to Himself.

The theological concept referred to as common grace points to instances of God revealing Himself even in the ordinary experiences of life. It is an invigorating way of viewing a world that can too easily leave us jaded and despairing. When we choose to see the world filled with God's presence, we will want to be a part of that glorious reality.

Consider still another conspiracy theory: "God causes everything to work together for the good of those who love God" (Rom. 8:28). Christians have often misquoted this verse—trying to make it say that everything will go well for us if we follow God or use it to make sense of a tragedy or disappointment—but in reality it reflects a healthy anti-paranoia. And when we look at it in this way, anti-paranoia sounds a lot like faith. God is in charge, at work in our world, though often behind the scenes. And most of all, He loves us. The conspiracy is working.

The Whole Universe Dancing

The English science-fiction writer Douglas Adams has one of his characters confronting the most astounding music on board an alien spacecraft. According to Adams' story, the music comes from a super computer able to convert the pulse and energy of all life on earth into a purely musical form. The music was somehow both amazingly complex and confoundingly simple but, above all, incredibly joyous and beautiful. The character later described the music: "Such music . . . I'm not religious, but if I were I would say it was a glimpse into the mind of God. Perhaps it was and I ought to be religious. I have to keep reminding myself that they didn't create the music, they only created the instrument which could read the score. And the score was life itself" *(Dirk Gently's Holistic Detective Agency)*.

In a similar vein, C. S. Lewis described the universe as a grand dance with our small planet as the only fragment of the vast swirling mass that is out of step. God created this huge spinning outpouring of life, beauty, and joy. The awesome scale of His creative power is the most obvious demonstration of God's greatness. Lewis suggests that "God carried in His hand a little object like a nut, and that . . . was 'all that is made'" *(The Four Loves)*.

The apparent ease with which the Lord brought "all that was made" into being dwarfs the magnitude of His creative work. "The Lord merely spoke, and the heavens were created. He breathed the word, and all the stars were born" (Ps. 33:6). For God, creating the largest solar system to the most bizarre or beautiful creatures to the smallest grain of sand was as simple as breathing is to us.

However, to create such a multiplicity of beings and things was not enough. The still greater complexity lay in ordering the incredibly intricate web of interactions between all the components of the created world. God so ordered the sun and moon as to affect the oceans upon earth and to play a role in the lives of the microscopic creatures living in them. Innumerable interactions across the world reveal the perfection of the balance of life brought into being by an omniscient Creator.

However, He did not stop there in His creation. In the world around us we experience an awesome variety of colors, shapes, smells, textures, and tastes. It is obvious that God wanted to create not merely a world that worked but also one that was inherently beautiful and could be enjoyed. Thus He gave us—as a part of His creation—the ability to perceive the beauty around us.

"And but for our body one whole realm of God's glory—all that we receive through our senses—would go unpraised. For the beast can't appreciate it and the angels are, I suppose, pure intelligences. They understand colour and taste better than our greatest scientists; but have they retinas or palates? I fancy the 'beauties of nature' are a secret God has shared with us alone" (C. S. Lewis, *Letters to Malcolm: Chiefly on Prayer*).

The music of life is beautiful because God created it to be beautiful. Rather than one consistent note, which would probably suffice for filling the formless void for most practical purposes, He composed a symphony of intertwining variety, beauty, and joy. We have to keep reminding ourselves that we did not create this music—God did that. Nor did we produce the senses by which we perceive such beauty—again, God did that. The Lord brought into being a world filled with joy for us to enjoy—thus He originated joy itself.

In this joy we find some hints both as to what the world once was and, indeed, what the creation made new in eternity will be. As C. S. Lewis suggests, the beauty and goodness we experience on earth are only "the scent of a flower we have not found, the echo of a tune we have not heard, news from a country we have never visited" *(Weight of Glory)*.

The Problem of Joy

One of the most common objections to Christianity is what people often refer to as the problem of pain. The question is how could pain exist—and particularly how can apparently good people suffer it—in a world ruled by a good, loving, and all-powerful God. Because pain obviously exists, therefore it is impossible to believe in the God asserted by Christians. It is a vexing question, and many writers have sought to defend Christianity by meeting the question head on—with varying degrees of success.

However, those who want to disprove, discount, or discard God themselves face a problem possibly even more difficult to explain. It involves the good things in life—the joy and the beauty. Rather than asking "Why do bad things happen to good people?" (by which we probably mean us), we can just as legitimately ponder "Why do good things happen to bad people?" (which can also refer to us). Countless instances of inexplicable joy, beauty, and variety surround us. The world would be much simpler and would conceivably operate just as well without all of them.

For example, rather than the 850 species of birds in Australia (as listed in the *Field Guide to Australian Birds*), a half dozen generic species of birds would surely suffice. Similarly, the variety of colors, aromas, and tastes found in a selection of fruit or vegetables might seem unnecessary in practical terms. If we only pause to observe, we will find an astounding range of trees, fish, insects, rocks, and almost any other category we might choose. Or the world could easily be black and white, and we—not knowing any better—would get along quite satisfactorily. After all, some animals such as cats do not see color at all, and they do fine.

There often seem no functional or practical reasons for so much of the beauty and sources of joy surrounding us in our everyday lives. And if we try to explain the world without God, then we also have to account for the abundance and even inefficiency of beauty.

Yes, both the philosophical and experiential problems of pain continue to persist—as well as the issue of why we find beauty even in a world filled with so much suffering. Speaking of the natural world, C. S. Lewis asks: "How can it be so beautiful and also so cruel, wasteful and futile?" However, even the apparent futility of so much of the natural world itself raises the question of the temporary beauty. For example, why does an insect living for less than 24 hours have such delicate and finely detailed wings? If one is to explain the world, as it actually presents itself to us, we cannot ignore its goodness and beauty.

The difference is how we see it. As poet Elizabeth Barrett Browning puts it: "Earth's crammed with heaven, and every common bush afire with God; but only he who sees takes off his shoes; the rest sit around it and pluck blackberries." Creator of the hidden colors in coral reefs, the fragile wings of butterflies, and the spectacular glory of the sunset, He is a God of both endless repetition and endless variety, but above all a God of endless beauty and joy.

Although we now catch only glimpses of beauty, joy, and glory, they still speak of boundless beauty, joy, and goodness beyond the tragedies of our world. Maybe the universe is not as silent and solemn as we often imagine: "We are perhaps permitted tragedy as a sort of merciful comedy: because the frantic energy of divine things would knock us down like a drunken farce. We can take our own tears more lightly than we could take the tremendous levities of the angels. So we sit perhaps in a starry chamber of silence, while the laughter of the heavens is too loud for us to hear" (G. K. Chesterton).

Joy Bubbling Over

S ome years ago my wife and I spent a year working as volunteer pastors in Tennant Creek, a tiny town situated in the center of the Northern Territory in outback Australia. We worked with a small group of church members in that area and involved ourselves in the youth center operated by the local community.

Each Thursday night we helped run a basketball competition that attracted many of the young people and children. The older kids would play basketball while the younger ones amused themselves in other ways.

One evening I sat observing the various games. Almost directly in front of me were two 8-year-old Aboriginal girls playing together. Their interaction was infectiously joyous, and I watched them for some time. Their main game consisted of simply standing with their faces only a few inches apart with the object being not to laugh. Although they continued it for a long time, each round within the game was surprisingly short-lived before yet another wave of laughter would bubble up from inside one or both of the little girls.

Compared to other Australians, "by virtually every test on the range of usually accepted social indicators such as rates of unemployment, rates of custody, rates of infant mortality, life expectancy, household income and other indicators, Aboriginal . . . individuals and communities are now, and have been in the past, at a serious disadvantage" (Council for Aboriginal Reconciliation). In addition to such social limitations, these children were quite small for their age and residents of an isolated community that offered little prospect of any dramatic improvement in their lives and those of their families. In spite of that, though, the pure joy of these two tiny girls was irrepressible.

That is how God intended life to be. He created it to have more joy in it. However, to attempt to discover what the world was like when God first created it by looking at what we now see around us is similar to trying to determine what a motorcar looks like when the only example available is one that has been in a serious accident. The present world is twisted, broken, and in some respects resembles nothing of its original condition. However, we are able to find some hints both as to what the world once was and, indeed, what the creation made new in eternity will be like.

To appreciate the true joy of creation—a joy and pride that God Himself felt—our challenge is somehow to see back to the moment of Creation. In his book *Disappointment With God* Philip Yancey tells the story of a famous English naturalist who fell asleep while sheltering from a storm. When the naturalist awoke, he found himself being watched by a small fox so young that it had not yet learned to be afraid of humans. The tiny animal picked up a bone, and, instinctively, the naturalist grabbed the other end, leading to a playful tug-of-war between the old man and the young fox. The naturalist suggested that this game was "the gravest, most meaningful act I shall ever accomplish. It was, in reality, a child's universe, a tiny and laughing universe." As he considered this story Yancey concluded that "despite the awesome emptiness, despite the pain that haunts it, something lingers, like a scent of old perfume." "At the heart of the universe is a smile, a pulse of joy passed down from the moment of creation."

We can still sense something of the joy that God created in the world around us, but it is in attempting to see how things were originally that allows us to get the best glimpse of the original joy. We are told that Adam and Eve enjoyed direct communion with God. In it they must have found their greatest joy as He shared the joy of the whole creation with them.

"In Bible study we start as flies on the wall, watching God deal with people of the past, overhearing His words to them and theirs to Him, noting the outcome of their faithful or faithless living. But then we realize that the God whom we were watching is watching us, that we too are wholly in His hands and that we are no less called and claimed by Him than were the Bible characters" (J. I. Packer, *Truth & Power: The Place of Scripture in the Christian Life*).

The relationship that the Creator originally had with Adam and Eve is the same one that He wants to have with us. The reason the Son of God came to this earth to die for our sins was to restore that connection. It is in such a close relationship with God that we will find our greatest joy.

I recently came across an interview of a producer working on a new album for one of the world's best-known musical groups. When asked what the musicians sought to accomplish in their recording, he answered, "The only thing that is appearing as a theme is an attempt to do the most difficult thing in music, which is to create joy. That is extremely hard. It's actually dead easy to make melancholy. It's easy to make energy, it's easy to make cleverness, it's easy to make intrigues, it's easy to make glamour. But it's very very hard to make joy. To make music that really grips you and lifts you in some way. That's hard."

The difficulty is that we cannot manufacture true joy whenever we want to. Genuine joy is the result of something much bigger than we. Though often difficult to discover in the world around us, we can find it within ourselves as a fruit of God living and working in our lives.

Such joy is not simply happiness, which is often based on such external circumstances as whether things are going well for us. Neither is it some insane ability to smile and giggle our way through the difficulties and tragedies life brings to us. Rather, whatever our circumstances, we experience an underlying joy through the goodness of God and the certainty of His victory over sin.

"Life in Christ . . . is a life of joy; above all else, such joy is to characterize the Christian community" (Gordon D. Fee, *Paul, the*

Spirit, and the People of God). God designed life to be full of joy—to be lived in a close relationship with Him. Such a relationship with God, and His power working in our lives, provide the root and the branch upon which the fruit of joy will grow.

However, that relationship will not be fully realized until God completely re-creates the world. Only then will the original joy that He established in the beginning once more be ours.

A Postcard of Grace

As I spent a quiet afternoon at a friend's place a few years ago I leafed through a large art book—perhaps the next best thing to wandering the halls of a major art gallery—and sometimes better, since it has the possibility of collecting paintings from around the world in a single volume. Flicking through the pages, I found myself struck by a particular painting: Salvador Dali's *The Sacrament of the Last Supper*.

The realism of Dali's treatment of this familiar scene surprised me. My knowledge of his talents involved little more than an awareness of his depiction of melting clocks and burning giraffes. Now this painting's sense of reality grabbed my attention. It shows Jesus as a young man. The animation in His portrayal not only drew me in but at the same time suggested something special about this Man—an inherent divinity.

And, coming from the brush of Dali, the scene is not a darkened upper room. In the background we see across a lake surrounded by hills. The view has fishing boats and a golden sky. Somehow the painting speaks of both humility and grandeur in the same breath.

Although I kept looking through the book, I returned again and again to the Dali painting. The following week I found a local framing shop and ordered a cheap print of the work. When it arrived a couple weeks later, I had it laminated. It then occupied a central position on my lounge room wall.

Two years later, however, I took the painting down, packed it in a box, and left it behind as we headed off around the world—first stop: Washington, D.C. Between working and other adventures we took the opportunity to explore many of the museums and art galleries that dot the United States capital. One afternoon, while selecting postcards in the gift shop of the National Gallery of Art, my wife drew my attention to one depicting Dali's *Last Supper.*

"Is that here?" I asked with rising excitement. Looking more closely at the postcard, I discovered it was indeed listed as a part of the museum's collection. In fact, we were standing in the gallery that housed it.

"Do you think we can see it?" I asked eagerly.

Since it was only 15 minutes to closing time, we hurriedly bought our postcards—including a number of this particular painting—and headed to the nearest information desk. Thrusting the postcard at the attendant, I asked directions. We had to go back through the gift shop to the far end of the building, down two escalators, around to the right, and into a small elevator lobby. And the single exhibit in that room was *the* painting—*The Sacrament of the Last Supper* by Salvador Dali.

It was huge. Until now I had only seen it in a book, poster-size on my wall, and recently on a postcard. But the painting that filled the wall in front of us was stunning. It was one of those moments in life of joyous surprise. The painting had surpassed all expectations, and that complete unexpectedness made the experience more overwhelming. We spent the next few minutes—before the gallery closed—in that room. During my five-month trip this was one of the true highlights—a moment of absolute grace.

In 1 Corinthians 13 Paul talks about seeing partially and then completely and the difference that makes (verse 12). Although we often quote the verse in relationship to the hurt and pain of life—and it fits well—it actually appears in the context of understanding love. It's as if we now receive only postcard-size pictures of the grace, the joy, and the goodness that await us in life.

Yet even the postcards can be almost overwhelming—that afternoon in the National Gallery of Art, for example. We can only imagine how much more astounding is the big picture of God's grace and the true, complete joy of life.

But with each new glimpse of goodness we find ourselves changed. The poster on my wall is now not just a picture—it is also a reminder of an experience of grace.

An Audience
of One

Acouple hours every week during a
four-year period I would shut myself
in a small room of a building in a back street
in suburban Townsville and talk. While in the
room alone and facing a blank wall, I spoke to
a potential audience of up to 200,000 people. It would be somewhat
presumptuous to claim that all 200,000 ever listen to Townsville's
Christian radio station Live FM, but even scaling the listener figures
back to the thousands who may tune in on any given day, it would be
quite a crowd if they tried to fit into the one tiny broadcast studio.

It can at times be almost as difficult and daunting to address one-
self to such a potentially wide variety of listeners in the course of the
broadcast. Both the physical and technological distance between the
presenter's microphone and the home, office, car, or workshop in
which the broadcast reaches the listener can create a considerable degree of impersonality. According to those who know such things,
the trick is to imagine you are speaking with a friend—to conduct a
one-sided conversation for an audience of one. In that way each of
the listeners can begin to feel as if you are talking just to them.

I was interested recently to discover that this echoes a Puritan
belief of how we should live our lives: "They lived as if they stood
before an audience of One. They carried on their lives as if the
only one whose opinion mattered were God" (Dallas Willard, *The
Divine Conspiracy*).

It is an attitude presented in the Bible in relationship both to our sins and to our good works. Psalm 139 sets out a detailed account of God's watch over every aspect of our lives—from our formation in the womb to our day-by-day existence. God's "thoughts about me . . . are innumerable!" (verse 17). According to David, we live each day with a loving and all-encompassing audience of One.

Against a background of such a faith and relationship with God, it hardly surprises us that when David found himself confronted about his adultery with Bathsheba, his immediate confession was "I have sinned against the Lord" (2 Sam. 12:13). This does not discount the others hurt by his actions—particularly Uriah and Bathsheba—but is an admission by Israel's king of the preeminent importance of his relationship with God. The primary pain caused by David's sin was the harming of his relationship with God. He is even more exclusive in his focus in Psalm 51 as he again reflects on this same sin: "Against you, and you alone, have I sinned" (verse 4).

Jesus taught a similar thing in Matthew 6, but this time in relationship to the good things we might do. He spoke about giving to the needy and about prayer and fasting. In each instance Jesus cautions against doing such things for public show and applause. Rather we should do them without fanfare and then "your Father, who knows all secrets, will reward you" (verse 4). Again, it is not that what we do has no impact on others but that we are playing for a much more significant Audience.

Such a realization can profoundly impact how we live our lives. The realization of our nakedness before the eye of God can be a daunting thought. When David says to God, "You have examined my heart and know everything about me" (Ps. 139:1), we flinch—and if we don't, we should. But God is not a harsh critic—rather, He is the loving Father. When we accept what He has done for us in Jesus and His death for us, it restores us to our right relationship with God as His children, and we can rejoice with David when he writes, "You both precede and follow me. You place your hand of blessing on my head" (verse 5). Your audience of one is the God who loves you, who died for you, and who wants to live with you forever: it is this God who loves you infinitely, who watches you intently.

In a world in which we find ourselves buffeted by countless voices and judged by innumerable measures, we are reminded there is only one Audience and one Judge who counts. Both the good and the evil we do have a different measure from that of the world around us. When we pray with David, "Search me, O God, and know my heart" (verse 23), we are not only acknowledging this Audience but also praying a prayer that releases us from many of the external pressures on our lives and choices. As Shakespeare suggested, all the world may be a stage—but the preeminent audience is an audience of One.

Commandment Number 1

Afew years ago—after 20-plus years growing up a Christian—I discovered what it was really to love God. Until then it had been a puzzling concept. I had no problem with believing in a deity and accepting His immensity and awesome power. It made sense that we should respect, obey, and probably worship such a being. However, loving such a huge God—probably incompletely described as the all-encompassing Force—did not follow quite so automatically.

Often when people talk about a relationship with God they are emphasizing that *knowing about* Him is not enough—*knowing* Him is the aim. Such knowing is an important step, and continuing growth in our knowledge of God is vital to a maturing relationship with Him. However, truly experiencing God is another step up. As Kevin Hart explains, "mystics are not so much concerned with *knowing* God as with *loving* Him" *(The Trespass of the Sign).*

It is interesting to discover Jesus presenting us with a somewhat startling foundation for loving God. When asked what was the greatest commandment, He quoted Deuteronomy 6:5: "You must love the Lord your God with all your heart, all your soul, and all your mind" (Matt. 22:37). Reading this well-known verse in this way may strike us as peculiar—God actually *commands* us to love Him. However, it does provide something of an answer to my initial questions. As a first step, we should love God because He told us to. Finding love as the first step in obedience to Him puts a different slant on the whole obedience thing. We then see the rest of the commandments in a new light, one based on a love for God.

Another time while He was on earth Jesus and His disciples were traveling to Jerusalem. They stopped for lunch in a small village "where a woman named Martha welcomed them into her home. Her sister, Mary, sat at the Lord's feet, listening to what he taught. But Martha was worrying over the big dinner she was preparing" (Luke 10:38-40) and came to Jesus, complaining that her sister was not helping.

Jesus' reply sounds harsh—and it is possible we do not have the complete story. After all, someone did need to make lunch. But Jesus was making a point. He gently scolds Martha for letting herself get distracted by the little things. She obviously knew Jesus. They were friends, and it is possible she knew the food He liked—and that may have been what she was working on. Yet Jesus wanted to remind her that He was there for a more important reason than lunch. "There is really only one thing worth being concerned about. Mary has discovered it—and I won't take it away from her" (verse 42).

The Cloud of Unknowing is one of the classic works of Christian mysticism. The unknown author describes how Mary recognized the God-ness in Jesus, and it was that she sought. "Nothing she saw or heard could budge her, but there she sat, completely still, with deep delight, and an urgent love reaching out into that high cloud of unknowing that was between her and God." While Mary recognized Jesus as God and knew Him as a person, she needed to go another step up—to an urgent, reaching love for God.

However, the question then arises as to how such a love can become a reality in our own lives. Again we confront the problem of a God who appears very different and distant from us. The first step is finding out about Him and getting to know Him. We can employ a number of practical ways in which we can get to know God better. The most obvious one is simply to spend time with Him, communicating with Him in worship, His Word, and prayer. The rough equation is that as we get to know God better, to understand better who He is and what He has done for us and to allow the Holy Spirit to work in our lives, we will then love God simply as a response to His great love for us.

But it is not a matter of locking ourselves in a small room with a Bible and not coming out until we can create some kind of warm, fuzzy feeling for God. Feelings can be difficult and unpredictable. During times of deep emotion and feeling, love for God is not a problem. However, loving God is a practical thing. C. S. Lewis suggests that "faking" the feelings might be just as useful. "People are often worried. They are told they ought to love God. They cannot find any such feeling in themselves. What are they to do? The answer is . . . Act as if you did. Do not sit trying to manufacture feelings. Ask yourself, 'If I were sure that I loved God, what would I do?' When you have found the answer, go and do it" *(Mere Christianity)*.

Fortunately, searching for the answer is not that difficult. Jesus Himself gave us some pointers. He consistently taught that our love for God and our response to His love for us can find expression in how we treat other people. Jesus said, "I assure you, when you did it to one of the least of these my brothers and sisters, you were doing it for me" (Matt. 25:40). Serving others is important for our continuing experience with God.

Our love for God compels us both to sit quietly and reach out to Him—something that Jesus commended Mary for—and to take practical steps to reach out to those around us, something that Jesus' parable approved the "sheep" for doing.

Of course, relationships are much easier to develop when both parties are interested in establishing them. While it may require them to work out some practical matters, the mutual interest greatly enhances the prospect of a significant relationship between them. So the thing we should always remember in the context of a relationship with God is that He wants us to experience Him. Revelation 3:20—"Here I stand at the door and knock. If you hear me calling and open the door, I will come in, and we will share a meal as friends"—often gets used in the context of people accepting God for the first time. However, as Richard Foster points out, the invitation actually first went to people who were already Christians *(Celebration of Discipline)*.

God addressed the invitation to you. He wants to step up His relationship with you. Loving you in the ultimate sense, He *commands* that you love Him. You may know about God; you may even know God; but you must also love Him. Such love is the key to experiencing Him.

Because
Life Hurts

Crashing Alone

A few days ago we went mountain-biking. During lunch we had watched a video of extreme mountain-biking. It presented about 30 minutes of incredible bicycling stunts, tightly edited together and set to a pumping musical sound track. Then for light relief toward the end of the compilation the video presented snippets from the stunts that did not quite go so well, resulting in spectacular crashes and bone-jarring collisions. They provided the supposedly comic element to the serious business of biking. And we laughed at the ungainly and dramatic spills. As the unfortunate riders cartwheeled and catapulted away from their hurtling bikes, their pain became the highlight of the video.

Just an hour later we were at the top of a nearby mountain with three miles (five kilometers) of downhill dirt tracks in front of us. The track had been newly graded, with a loose covering of soil concealing any ruts. It was a warm and sunny day. The fine dust the first riders had kicked up hung in the afternoon light as we began our descent. We had little need to pedal, as the increasing slope gave us plenty of momentum. Every few hundred yards erosion bars crossed the road, playing the role of a large speed bump. The more confident riders ahead used them to launch themselves into the air, feeling the momentary freedom of flight.

But only a few minutes later another of those mounds was my undoing. My bike hit it at full speed and dug into the loose topsoil on landing. Instantly I found myself farther down the track than my fallen mount. The soft dust seemed to have cushioned my fall somewhat, and I lay there for a moment, half buried in the powdered dirt.

Because I had been riding last in the group, I was now alone. My fall had gone unobserved, and I faced no danger from following riders. Winded, it took me a few seconds to check my injuries. My hip, my chest, and my arm had all landed hard (the loose topsoil barely covered the much harder road base). Carefully I got to my feet. The afternoon was still warm, the sunlight still playing with the dust in the air—a little more of it now—and the track still beckoned. But I rode on only gingerly. It was not quite as entertaining as the extreme biking video had suggested.

Now, a couple days later, I am still moving a little slower than usual, I have some interestingly colored bruising, and it still hurts to laugh or sneeze. And now you are either laughing or wincing—but not experiencing.

"I think the most common human experience is being alone," someone once said. It was pop philosophy—perhaps a throwaway line—from a TV sitcom. While not necessarily a reliable source of worthwhile profundity, the line still stayed with me. And perhaps it was true.

Nowhere are we more alone than when we experience pain. It is the most isolating human experience. No matter how much we watch, read about, laugh at, or sympathize with the pain of others, pain itself is always a unique and isolated experience. There is simply no way anyone else can share our hurt, our sorrow, or our fear.

Reflecting on his own suffering and grief after the death of his wife, C. S. Lewis writes, "You can't really share someone else's weakness, or fear or pain. What you feel may be bad. It might conceivably be as bad as what the other felt. . . . But it would still be quite different" (A Grief Observed). He goes on to suggest that the closer we are to someone who is suffering, the more likely our experiences of a particular pain would be different from those of the other person. We will experience significantly different aspects of even the same pain.

Even trying to write about or read about pain is as limited as watching the crashes on the extreme mountain-biking highlights in comparison with the dusty, painful experience I had a little later that afternoon. The theory and observation of pain are never the same as the experience itself: "When pain is to be borne, a little courage helps more than much knowledge, a little human sympathy more than much courage, and the least tincture of the love of God more than all" (C. S. Lewis, *The Problem of Pain*).

And there lies the clue. In our isolation we stand completely alone before the God who loves us—a realization that brings with it both extreme joy and extreme terror. He knew us in our solitude before we even knew ourselves—"You watched me as I was being formed in utter seclusion" (Ps. 139:15). Despite the lonely darkness of our pain, He knows where we are: "And when I wake up in the morning"—sore and bruised though I might be—"you are still with me!" (verse 18).

Revisiting
the Tragedy

E very so often evil grabs our attention. Whether it is the death of someone close, a new human outrage, or yet another natural disaster, it shakes us from our happy or at least apathetic cohabitation with evil. While such evil naturally repulses us, at the same time it can be hard to imagine a world without it, without pain, and without sadness. Such things seem so much a part of our lives that we cannot conceive of the world any other way.

So we establish kind of a provisional truce with evil. Something like "If it doesn't bother us too much, we won't fight too hard against it." But that is a dangerous and delicate cease-fire in which evil never really ceases fire. We risk becoming so used to evil—and the seemingly endless succession of individual evil acts—that, because of the isolated nature of each instance of evil, "everything is pardoned in advance and therefore everything is cynically permitted" (Milan Kundera, *The Unbearable Lightness of Being*).

The answer to this insidious apathy toward the evil in the world is simply to pause to consider the overwhelming tragedy it causes. This does not have to be a morbid descent into a hope-destroying horror. Rather, sometimes we should stop trying to rationalize and explain the evil we experience and see around us. Frederick Buechner compares this with watching the television news with the sound turned off. "The news with . . . no words to explain it or explain it away, no words to cushion or sharpen the shock of it, no definition given to dispose of it. . . . Just the thing itself, life itself, or as much as the screen can hold" *(Telling the Truth)*.

We can also have a similar experience in revisiting the story of what the world was once like and how it lost its original condition. The story is well known, even if only as the "myth" of Adam and Eve. Reading stories we have heard many times before brings a risk that we will miss the real tragedy and drama of the event related—that we become too used to it and no longer respond to its meaning. We face such a danger with the story of the entrance of evil into our world. However, the account of Adam and Eve's disobedience to God's command when they ate the fruit of the single forbidden tree (Gen. 3:1-10) is one of the saddest stories ever told.

I was recently reminded of the real tragedy it portrayed when I read John Milton's *Paradise Lost*. The poem beautifully portrays the creation of this new and pure world. It led me to appreciate in a new way God's involvement and interaction with His new creation and particularly with Adam and Eve. Milton's re-creation of these wonderful scenes is a work of incredible imagination.

His description of exquisite beauty and joy sets the scene for the horrific tragedy that is the Fall. The newly created world—and the reader—almost hold their collective breaths as they watch the temptation and the first sin. It is a heartbreaking moment.

One of the significant themes of the grand poem is the loss of Adam and Eve's innocence. As Milton puts it, "innocence, that as a veil/Had shadow'd them from knowing ill, was gone,/ . . . naked left/To guilty shame" *(Paradise Lost*, Book IX, lines 1054-1058).

Such loss of innocence is the basis for the greatest suffering of the Fall: humanity's separation from God, told poignantly in Genesis 3:8-10. Instead of the friendship Adam and Eve had once enjoyed with Him they now hid themselves in their attempt to escape His presence.

When we pause to look at just the thing itself, we find that separation from God was—and continues to be—evil's greatest consequence. It is a tragedy worth considering in the context of our often apathetic toleration of the evil lurking in our world and our lives.

Suffering's Glorious Unanswer

Unfortunately, suffering is an inescapable part of life as we know it. Every age and culture has debated its possible reasons. However, the Judeo-Christian belief in an all-powerful, all-wise, and all-good God gives the question greater philosophical and theological urgency. The difficulty is to maintain this belief in the face of the actual experience of intense human suffering. Dealing with this is the impulse driving the book of Job.

The majority of the book consists of debate between Job, his three friends, and Elihu as to the cause of the patriarch's sufferings. They also consider, in a broader sense, the apparent anomaly of the righteous suffering and the wicked prospering: "The great question is raised more by the distribution of suffering than by its existence" (Theodore H. Robinson, *The Poetry of the Old Testament*).

However, to simply read Job as an attempt to answer even these pressing questions is to miss its theological point. The prologue of chapters 1 and 2 provides an insight to the story unknown by any of the human voices of the remainder of the book. The reader's extra knowledge does provide a partial answer to some of the questions Job and his friends raise—but even then it is still incomplete.

The narrative prologue succinctly sets up the problem of suffering. It introduces Job as a man who "was blameless, a man of complete integrity. He feared God and stayed away from evil" (Job 1:1).

He had seven sons and three daughters and great wealth. However, verses 13–19 narrate a day in which all his wealth and his children vanish in a succession of disasters.

In the midst of his grief Job's response is to worship God and, with an air of resignation, to admit that "the Lord gave me everything I had, and the Lord has taken it away" (verse 21). However, worse was yet to come for Job, and he soon comes down with a painful skin disease. The patriarch finds himself reduced to sitting on a rubbish heap, scraping his painful skin with a broken piece of pottery. It is the position his three friends find him in and forms the backdrop for the debate that follows. Job experiences such anguish that the opening of the debate involves seven days of silence in which "no one said a word, for they saw that his suffering was too great for words" (Job 2:13).

Their silence is the most sympathetic thing the friends ever do. Otherwise the reactions of those around him intensify his suffering. Indeed, the despair of his wife, the accusations of his friends, and the apparent silence of God contribute more to Job's pain than his physical predicament. The patriarch laments that his friends are estranged and what is left of his family has forgotten him (Job 19:13, 14). He is misunderstood, unanswered, and—as his friends' frustration grows—even abused.

After his period of silence, Job launches into his bitter complaint: "a cry of anguish from a soul quivering with agony" (E.S.P. Heavenor, "Job," *New Bible Commentary*). He questions both the justice of what he is going through and, more broadly, the apparent undeserved sufferings of the righteous in the world while the wicked often appear to prosper. The patriarch weaves the two questions together throughout his arguments. His present agony gives urgency to what were previously theoretical problems. Ironically, the answer assumed by his friends and even Job himself adds mental anguish to his physical distress.

That answer underlies the tension in the narrative and debate of the book of Job. "The theory dominant at the time this immortal poem was written was that suffering is the infallible index of personal culpability" (H. R. Minn, *The Book of Job*). Considering the rest of the Old Testament, the existence of such a belief was hardly surprising. God had repeatedly promised to the emerging Hebrew nation that if they followed His ways they would prosper, and would defeat their enemies. Alternatively, if they did not, He would not protect them, and disaster would then come upon them. The book of Proverbs also emphasizes such reasoning.

Accordingly, ancient society would expect that if Job was righteous, he would be blessed and, if he was wicked, he would be punished. His friends naturally concluded that Job's predicament must be indicative of his sin: "This is the fate that awaits the wicked. It is the inheritance decreed by God" (Job 20:29). Eliphaz chides Job, as someone who has often encouraged others, for being dismayed: "But now when trouble strikes, you faint and are broken" (Job 4:5). The friends repeatedly urge the patriarch to confess his sin to God and seek His forgiveness and reinstatement to favor.

They become increasingly frustrated as he continues to assert his innocence. Eliphaz expresses their exasperation: "Is not your wickedness great? Are not your sins endless?" (Job 22:5, NIV). He affirms that God upholds the righteous who see the destruction of the wicked "and rejoice" (verse 19, NIV).

So strong is Job's friends' belief in this answer to his questions that they charge him with blasphemy in rejecting divine justice: "But why should I condemn you? Your own mouth does!" (Job 15:6) Eliphaz charges. Even if he has not sinned in the past, he is now sinning against God by his vehement denial of his sinfulness and his affirmation of his own self-righteousness.

Despite the pressure from his friends, Job refuses to accept their formula. While he admits the apparent truth of their theory (Job 9:2; 26:3; see also 6:25 and 12:3)—and it seems he would have himself employed such reasoning before his suffering—he cannot reconcile this with the reality of his own situation.

Initially Job curses the day of his birth and longs for death to spare him his agony. He recognizes that justifying himself is self-defeating—"Though I am innocent, my own mouth would pronounce me guilty" (Job 9:20)—but passionately maintains his innocence of any sin deserving such trials as he endures.

For Job, his suffering calls into question God's nature. The patriarch faces a difficult dilemma: "If God is almighty, then he is not just; if God is just, then he is not almighty" (Ackerman, Jenks, Jenkinson, and Blough, *Teaching the Old Testament in English Classes*). Job does not question the Lord's omnipotence. Both his friends and he himself affirm the divine greatness and power. Rather Job suggests that God is not just and that He has for some unknown reason particularly targeted him, like a lion hunting its prey (Job 10:16).

Job's reaction to his conclusion makes unsteady progress throughout the dialogue. At first he wishes he were dead, then asks God to leave him alone to live his short life in peace. But gradually he becomes bolder and expresses his desire to reason with God, even if it kills him. Job believes that if he could receive a fair hearing, he would be able to justify himself before God. The imagery switches between Job appealing to God, Job accusing God, and Job defending himself before God.

The patriarch's conclusions are a hope that he will indeed see the Lord one day—whether in this life or after death (Job 19:25, 26)—and the assurance that he has a Witness in heaven and an Advocate on high (Job 16:19). Job is certain that he will be justified when he gets a chance to present his case. In this way he affirms his faith in a just ordering of the universe and ultimately a just God despite all external appearances.

Then—much to the surprise of Job and his friends—God Himself enters the discussion. However, the most startling feature of the divine response to the patriarch's complaint is that God does not provide an answer to any of his questions or complaints except whether or not He would answer him. Philip Yancey suggests that "God could have read a page from the phone book and Job would have meekly consented" (*The Bible That Jesus Read*). Indeed, the divine speech, though a grand discourse, adds little to that already considered in the preceding chapters: Job, Zophar, and Elihu have acknowledged God's control of the natural world and the universe. The most important aspect of God's response is simply that He did answer.

God's appearance and declarations awe Job into silence. He admits that he spoke of things that "I did not understand, things far too wonderful for me" (Job 42:3) and repents of his charges against God. The Lord rebukes Job's friends and instructs the patriarch to pray for their forgiveness. However, God accepts Job and affirms what the reader has known from the beginning—that the man is blameless and has spoken "what is right" (verse 7, NIV).

The book offers no direct answer to the problem of suffering. However, it does regard the assurance that God is in charge of the universe and the affirmation of Job's faith as sufficient. "The problem of human suffering grows small when . . . man understands that he is not the center of the universe around whom everything revolves. . . . He does not know and does not need to know why he suffers, for he has been accorded a vision of God" (Julius A. Bewer, *The Literature of the Old Testament*).

The reader has witnessed the dialogue and debate of the preceding 40 chapters with background knowledge of the meetings in heaven between God and Satan in chapters 1 and 2. But as for Job, even at the conclusion of his experience he still has no knowledge of the bigger picture behind the suffering he has endured.

However, he and his friends have come close to the real answer. On a number of occasions the question has risen as to whether Job's righteousness or wickedness or questions can ever have any significance to God (Job 22:3; 23:6; 35:7). The insight of chapters 1 and 2 suggests that an individual's faith and actions can and do matter to the Lord. In a kind of bet, "God was letting his own reputation ride on the response of a single human being" (Yancey, *The Bible That Jesus Read*).

Throughout the anguished and frustrated discussion of suffering we find in the book of Job, the overriding theme is that a person's response to suffering and, ultimately, to God is more important than the reason behind whatever the present circumstance might be. As C. S. Lewis has Screwtape write—using the reverse demon logic— "Our cause is never more in danger than when a human, no longer desiring, but still intending, to do our Enemy's will, looks round upon a universe from which every trace of Him seems to have vanished, and asks why he has been forsaken, and still obeys" *(The Screwtape Letters)*.

Living Amid
the Headlines

 It was the kind of thing that leaves a person without anything to say—but about which so much is said. All of a sudden the word "Bali" was no longer a place but an event—a painful scar.

Writing in the days following the Bali terrorist bombing, ex-patriot Australian Clive James admitted that he was struggling to understand what had happened. "I owe it to my dead, wounded and bereaved countrymen to say straight away that I have no clear idea of what that conclusion will be. This is no time to preach, and least of all from a prepared text" (in *The Guardian,* Oct. 16, 2002).

Unlike James, I know what my conclusion will be: a reminder that God still loves us all and a conviction that somehow He is still in control. But, as James suggests, preaching often doesn't go particularly well in the face of such raw tragedy. I will not do that—rather, I intend to share some thoughts occurring to me as a young person living amid the headlines and trying to come to terms with the tragedies surrounding us all. So while the conclusion is already outlined, the path toward it might be a little less certain.

When we heard the news of the Bali bombing we were in New York. Knowing that we were Australian, someone mentioned that a bombing had occurred in Bali—and many Australians were missing. Late on that Saturday night we visited Times Square. We paused and watched as the electronic tickers spelled out the early details of the far-off tragedy.

Interspersed with updates on the carnage in Bali was the latest on the Washington, D.C., sniper, at that time having claimed eight lives and bringing fear to streets, schools, and workplaces across a wide area. It was still another headline in which we—living and working in the Washington area—had a keen and horrified interest.

There was also the continuing talk of war against Iraq and other more forgettable headlines of that particular day. And, of course, about 50 city blocks away was the large hole in the ground that we visited the next day. It marked the spot where a little more than a year before the twin towers of the World Trade Center had once stood. Feeling the scars of that tragedy is now simply a part of being in New York City.

The inclement night caught up the city's lights and reflected them back on the wet streets, the low clouds, and even the murky rain itself. Amid the damp fug of neon and drizzle, the racing, lurid headlines belied the somber and heart-wrenching questions they prompted.

Reflecting again on those questions, I remembered the beautifully plaintive cover version of the Tom Waits' song "Georgia Lee" I had heard just a few days previously. The bustling concert space had been stilled almost to the point of tears by the three haunting questions of the chorus: "Why wasn't God watching?" "Why wasn't God listening?" "Why wasn't God there?"

Such questions are not just the philosophical musings of a stylishly disaffected poet—they are the cries of our hearts that recur with each new tragedy, each new headline. Tragedy prompts us to reach out—even if at the same time we again question whether there is anything or anyone to reach out to.

The *Courier-Mail* told of a similar moment in Brisbane's landmark Storey Bridge Hotel on Sunday afternoon, a week after the Bali attack. Friends of victim Jodie Cearns gathered to pray for her recovery. A priest among them began reciting the Lord's Prayer. "The whole pub fell suddenly still," the *Courier-Mail* reported, "as not only Jodie's friends joined in the prayer but hundreds of strangers as well." She died from her horrific injuries the following Tuesday night, leaving more sorrow and more questions.

Yet even in the midst of these anguished cries we can still hear the beginnings of answers. When we find ourselves repulsed by such suffering, we are admitting that this is not how things should be—and perhaps suggest that the world as we see and experience it is not all there is to life. When we ask why God wasn't listening or watching or seemed absent, we express our almost subconscious belief that He should have been there. And when we pray, we express a belief—however tentative it may be—that somewhere, somehow, Someone might be listening.

While some might dismiss what happened that Sunday afternoon in the corner bar of the Storey Bridge Hotel as simply an expression of communal grief in a cultural form that we might expect in a society with a still-lingering Christian heritage, there may well be something more to it than that. Perhaps this form of reaching out to God is an appropriate human response, no matter what the culture or heritage.

The primary significance of the prayer we know as the Lord's Prayer is that God gave it to us Himself. But it was not the Lord thundering on an Old Testament mountain and handing down a prayer written in stone for us to obey. Instead, it was Deity in the form of humanity—Jesus, who lived on this earth as a man, who experienced pain, tragedy, grief, and disappointment. As such, the prayer Jesus taught His friends to pray was one specifically fitted to the dual realities of sorrow and hope.

Jesus was God with human feelings. One of the startling features of His own suffering during His crucifixion and death was that this was God questioning and even doubting God. G. K. Chesterton points to Jesus' cry from the cross—"My God, my God, why have you forsaken me?" (Matt. 27:46)—and suggests that in all the world's religions we can find "only one divinity who ever uttered their isolation; only one religion in which God seemed for an instant to be an atheist" (Orthodoxy). This is the Jesus who gave this prayer to His followers—and to the Christian tradition since—a God who understands our perspective, our deepest heart-wrenching cries.

So when we pray—as the crowd did that Sunday afternoon at the Storey Bridge Hotel—"May your kingdom come soon. May your will be done here on earth just as it is in heaven" (Matt. 6:10), the first component of the prayer is an admission and acknowledgment that God's kingdom and will are not yet complete and present realities in our world. The goodness and beauty we see around us do offer us glimpses of these realities, but they are only glimpses—as yet.

As yet—here we encounter the second component of the prayer: the looking and longing for something better. We pray for more of those glimpses, for more of the reality of God's kingdom and His will to be seen in our lives and in our world. But that doesn't mean that we have to understand everything about Him and what our reaching out in this way might mean. It is enough simply that we do it.

And we also look for an ultimate answer. In response to the question of how the righteous should respond to headlines proclaiming nearly overwhelming tragedy and evil apparently triumphant, David wrote—and perhaps sang—"The Lord is still in his holy temple; he still rules from heaven. He closely watches everything that happens here on earth. . . . God is good, and he loves goodness; the godly shall see his face" (Ps. 11:4-7, TLB).

That's what God was doing on earth. Jesus was not just here on a fact-finding trip or even a missionary endeavor. He had come to make a way to fix the tragedy and evil in our world. Through His seemingly God-forsaken and shattering death He paid the incredible price difference between a world gone horribly wrong and one made new. And He did it because of God's amazing and overwhelming love for us. Amid the headlines that make up life in our world, that love still remains.

When we pray the prayer Jesus taught, whether in a pub, a church, or in our hearts, we are—in a way—lodging our vote for that love to reclaim its rightful place as the ruling impulse in our lives and in our world. It is this reality that gives me hope amid the headlines. God still loves us all, and somehow He is still in control.

Deliver Us From Evil

It is not hard to find evil. It seeks us out. Both in big and small ways it seems simply a part of the very fabric of our lives and of our world. However, when confronted by the big acts of horror, we remember—if we have had any opportunity to forget—the real magnitude of the problem of evil.

It reminds us also of the significance of Jesus' direction that we should pray, "Deliver us from evil" (Matt. 6:13, KJV).

Evil in the World: Without wanting to downplay recent tragedies such as the Pacific Ocean tsunami, the well-publicized disasters are only examples of the countless lesser-known ones around the world. On personal, local, national, and international levels, each day's list of tragedies extends far beyond those trumpeted in the news headlines.

When we personally encounter the menace of evil, we pray with David, "End the wickedness of the ungodly, but help all those who obey you" (Ps. 7:9). It is a prayer echoed throughout the Bible and by God's people throughout history.

Such events also give a new perspective on our relationship to the evil in our world. Faced with the almost overwhelming sense of evil, we can appreciate Paul's exhortation to "hate what is wrong. Stand on the side of the good" (Rom. 12:9).

When events so brutally remind us of the true nature of evil, it should also inspire us again to fight evil in all its forms in our world. We must work toward building justice, mercy, grace, and peace within and beyond our personal spheres of influence.

And we pray: "Deliver us from evil."

Evil in Ourselves: Yet when we turn from the world and its evil and honestly look at ourselves, we find little comfort.

"You and I are not, at bottom, so different from these ghastly creatures" (C. S. Lewis, letter, Apr. 16, 1940). While Lewis was commenting on Hitler and Stalin, the principle applies more broadly. A part of our horror at the evil we see in the world is the recognition of at least the seeds of that same demonic element in ourselves. True, we can identify with the victims—"it could have been any one of us"—but we can also recognize with horror our own potential role as perpetrators of evil.

Even more than that, our evil is not just potential—in many different ways, large and small, it is intensely real in us. Paul described the battle with the evil within: "It seems to be a fact of life that when I want to do what is right, I inevitably do what is wrong" (Rom. 7:21). It is an ongoing, frustrating, but essential struggle.

The fact that evil is everywhere makes it easy to become almost comfortable with its influence. But we should never ignore it in any way. God did not create or destine us to be part of a world filled with evil. "So get rid of all the filth and evil in your lives, and humbly accept the message God has planted in your hearts, for it is strong enough to save your souls" (James 1:21).

So we pray: "Deliver us from evil."

The Ultimate Deliverance: And there is yet another sense in which we pray "Deliver us from evil." Perhaps the Lord's Prayer has summed it up earlier: "May your kingdom come soon" (Matt. 6:10). But in our frustration and anguish, we cry out, "How long, O Lord?" (Ps. 6:3).

Even if it seems so at times, heaven will not remain silent forever. Ultimately, evil has only one solution: Jesus Himself. He came to earth because of God's boundless love in response to the evil of this world. Our evil led to His crucifixion, but His death will also heal that same evil. He rose from the grave, signaling God's victory over evil in all its forms. Jesus will come again to destroy it completely. On that day—and forever afterward—evil will be no more. God will re-create both our world and each one of us.

Each new tragedy, each unfolding horror, each further appearance of evil, should call us back to Jesus and the hope we have in Him. In the face of such monstrous evil He is our only hope—and He will return.

When we pray with the closing words of the Bible, "Come, Lord Jesus" (Rev. 22:20), we are again praying: "Deliver us from evil."

The Prayer Flower

Prayer is a lot like radio broadcasting. We sit alone—perhaps in a small room—and talk to the wall in the hope that Someone, somewhere, is listening. Through a process and technology we barely understand we try to reach out to the unseen listener. Although we can prepare beforehand for the communication, as often as not it might be just as well to make it up as we go along. Perhaps sometimes the best arises from spontaneity. But on other occasions the progress is awkward, and we cannot even begin to imagine what might lie beyond the blank walls enclosing us.

Then, every so often, we receive a response, faint though it might be. A voice comes back—a message of encouragement or even criticism. The important thing is that it briefly reassures us that someone is out there. But that someone—or Someone—is all-important.

It is perhaps most difficult to reach beyond our tiny bare-walled rooms, to hope for anything or Anyone beyond them, during times of suffering and anguish. Then, even our prayers—our attempts to communicate with the "outside"—can add to our pain. Reflecting on his own experience of sorrow, C. S. Lewis comments: "And one prays; but mainly such prayers as are themselves a form of anguish" *(Letters to Malcolm: Chiefly on Prayer)*. When our prayers just seem to bounce back to us from the surrounding walls, the room feels smaller still, and the ricocheting pleas wound us further.

While in some ways suffering is easier for people of faith—having a hope and strength beyond themselves—in other ways belief makes it more complicated and difficult. The problem of pain is also a problem of faith—but only for those who already believe. "The 'hiddenness' of God perhaps presses most painfully on those who are in another way nearest to God" *(ibid.)*. For those of us who live in the expectancy of His presence and goodness, God's apparent absence and silence compound our pain and fear.

And there come moments when we are simply unable to believe, when a primitive nothingness seems our only visible option. Even then, by sheer force of will or habit we still cry out, in the style of Job, David's anguished psalms, and Jeremiah's lamentations, and in some incredible way our cry of hopelessness is still a prayer.

Robert McCrum was a successful London publishing executive who suffered a severe stroke at just 40 years of age. Despite his avowed atheism, he found himself reaching out to something in his periods of greatest desperation. "I pray to a God I don't believe in. But I had an absurd thought the other day, that the thing about God is that even if you don't believe in him, he listens to you" (McCrum, *My Year Off*).

It's a huge thought. Even during the moments when we are so hurt, grief-stricken, or frightened that we cannot see any way to reach out to God, He still hears those cries—and somehow, in His humility and graciousness, they can count as prayers. Maybe that's part of God's promise that "I will answer them before they even call to me" (Isa. 65:24). Before we are able to summon the willpower, the focus, the right words, or whatever we think we might need to pray "properly," God is already answering. In prayer, it seems, His readiness to listen is infinitely more important than our readiness to pray.

In his novel *Lilith* George MacDonald has one of his characters discover a tiny flower he is unable to identify. The character asks his traveling companion about the mysterious bloom. The raven tells him it is a unique prayer-flower: "Not one prayer-flower is ever quite like another." Its beauty, form, color, and scent overwhelm the story character. "I did see that the flower was different from any flower I had ever seen before," he reflects. "Therefore I knew I must be seeing a shadow of the prayer in it; and a great awe came over me to think of the heart listening to the flower."

That heart is the heart of God. The heartbeat that sustains the universe pauses to hear our stumbling, desperate, and even doubting cries.

An Unfinished Work

One of the interesting—and challenging—features of being a rookie teacher in a university is marking assignments. I recently received a first assignment from a first-year student, which, on an initial glance, did not create a good first impression. It had no title page or bibliography. The assignment consisted of one single-spaced sheet of paper. Across the top the student had written his name and student number in ballpoint ink. On top of this, it had come in more than a week past the due date.

Nevertheless, I approached it with a willingness to give credit for the good points it might have had. Unfortunately, it was difficult to find them. The conclusion of the essay only compounded my frustration. In the midst of a sentence that was not making much sense in any case, the typing simply stopped. I was bemused.

One of the other interesting features of teaching in a university is that there exists little direct training to qualify a person for such a position. To teach in high school, primary school, and even day care, an individual needs at least a diploma and sometimes up to four years of specialized education. However, to teach in a university one simply needs to have done well in studying the subject itself, irrespective of teaching ability. Thankfully, the lecturer in charge of the subject is usually happy to answer queries such as those raised by the assignment I had just read.

He cast an experienced eye across the paper, smirked, and suggested an appropriate response would be, "Were you suddenly attacked from behind and rendered unable to continue writing?" We guessed the computer word count may have reached the set word limit and—to this student—that may have seemed an obvious place to cease writing. I returned to my office and pondered what I should comment on it, trying to find a balance between the bitingly sarcastic and an expression of legitimate concern at the submission of such a piece of work.

After some consideration, I wrote—perhaps still a little too sarcastically—"Some of the arguments of this essay may have made more sense if the concluding sentence had been completed."

While the nonexistent second half of that final sentence may not have been sufficient to salvage that assignment, it is a useful way of thinking. It is too easy to judge something or someone without having the full story—and maybe we sometimes evaluate God in a similar way, before He has completed the final sentence.

When we look around us and within us at the problems, the pain, and the confusion that fill our lives, it can almost be a reflex action to blame God—or at least start questioning His goodness or His power or both. The problem with assessing God is that He is not finished yet. The Bible admits such incompleteness: "For we know that all creation has been groaning as in the pains of childbirth right up to the present time" (Rom. 8:22). That "all creation" includes us—disappointments are often a part of how things are at present.

It is interesting to note the comment at the end of the Bible's greatest discussion of faith. Having listed the faithfulness of many of the Old Testament heroes, it reads, "All of these people we have mentioned received God's approval because of their faith, yet none of them received all that God had promised" (Heb. 11:39). Put simply, God had not yet written the last sentence.

Right at the end of the Bible Jesus claims for Himself the titles of "the First and the Last, the Beginning and the End" (Rev. 22:13). While He is making a significant and all-encompassing claim, perhaps He is also admitting that the time in between is not quite so simple. But we have the assurance that He will have the final word.

The difficulty we have is that our present perspective is limited to the in-between time. It can feel a long way from our present circumstances to what God wants to do, but the Bible gives us an indication of and hope for how He will compose the final sentence. Until then we will always have some questions that need to wait for life's ultimate sentence to be completed.

Maybe, for a change, we should give God the benefit of the doubt. Perhaps somewhere in the last sentence things will begin to make a little bit more sense.

Because You
Can Make a
Difference

When the Good Samaritan Is Not Good Enough

Recently I conducted an afternoon program with a group of church young people. During it I asked them to act out in groups a practical expression of one beatitude. Despite assigning different verses within the Beatitudes to the respective groups, four of the five groups acted out stories loosely adapted from that of the parable of the good Samaritan, mostly involving helping people with vehicles broken down on the roadside. They did their impromptu adaptations creatively and with the best of intentions, but as an expression of the particular beatitudes—and of our Christian responsibility—they were somewhat misguided.

Without doubt the story of the good Samaritan is a powerful and worthy example of Christian good works. However, there comes a point when the good Samaritan is not good enough.

First—on a personal level—we need to extend our influence beyond the random and the opportunistic. If we limit the practical expressions of our Christianity to good-Samaritan-type instances, we may have extended periods in our lives when we do not see people broken down along the side of the road on our way to work or school. We run the risk of our good intentions being frustrated by an occasional lack of obvious "victims" in our immediate neighborhoods—or, for many of us, a lack of mechanical or other practical knowledge.

Rather we can make intentional and practical decisions to live lives more truly in harmony with the Beatitudes and the rest of the Bible's teachings about the Christian's social responsibilities. It happens at a deeper level than just brief moments of assistance to those we stumble across. The profound goodness at the heart of Jesus' teachings should pervade all aspects of our lives: how we treat others, how we live, where we live, what careers we choose, how we spend our money, what car we drive, how we relate to our communities, and how we respond to the big issues in our world. It involves far more than just random reactions to unfortunates we come into contact with.

The second point at which the example of the good Samaritan may fall short of the impact Christianity should be making in our world is at the systemic level. In many parts of the world the political, economic, social, and cultural systems inflict heartbreaking misery on people—almost invariably on the poorest and those least able to speak up for themselves. The appropriate Christian response to such systemic oppression is a part of what Jesus refers to as "the important things of the law—justice, mercy, and faith" (Matt. 23:23).

But it seems that Christians often do not feel comfortable addressing such issues—and those brave few who step up to challenge such systems or institutions find themselves under fire from both fellow Christians and the governments or corporations they seek to reform.

Tony Campolo refers to the good Samaritan when he questions the social order and infrastructure that allowed such exploitation. "When you minister to the poor of the world directly and individually," he comments, "even governments may lend you a hand. But begin suggesting that a government's political and economic systems actually create privation and suffering, and you will be told that you're in over your head—that you're messing around in areas that Christians ought to leave alone" (Tony Campolo, "Social Action," *Adventures in Missing the Point*).

Campolo quotes Brazilian bishop Donn Helder Camaro, who himself faced such a reality: "When I gave them food, they called me a saint. Yet when I asked why they had no food in the first place, they called me a Communist."

Yes, the good Samaritan is good, and we should be alert to good Samaritan opportunities. But as Christians we need to take intentional, informed, and focused steps to address ourselves, our resources, and our influences to helping our "neighbors" across the world.

Tolerance—Love in Overdrive

In his introduction to *The Retreat From Tolerance* Australian commentator Phillip Adams makes a frank admission. "I've been fighting bigotry for 50 years," he writes. "Does this smack of arrogance? Far from seeking to cast myself in an heroic light, that sentence is a confession. Let me now complete it. I've been fighting bigotry for 50 years—my own."

It's an admission that most of us can identify when we are honest with ourselves. We have a natural liking and inclination toward things that are familiar, people who look like us and think the way we do. And a natural dislike and inclination against anything different. An attitude of tolerance is the practical safeguard against abuse produced by such prejudices.

During the past couple decades Western society has come to regard intolerance as the last remaining "sin." Almost everything else, it seemed, could be allowed, justified, or excused, but intolerance was the peculiar vice of those who endeavored to maintain some form of morality.

The problem with this view of tolerance is that it misses the point. Tolerance is not an "anything goes as long as it doesn't hurt anybody else" attitude. Writer Clement F. Rogers summed up such a position when he asserted that "it is easy to be tolerant when you do not care." But that's not really tolerance—it's just carelessness.

And much of what people have passed off as tolerance in recent years is simply a moral lack.

Instead, those who show the greatest tolerance are those who have the most definite personal beliefs and morality, yet at the same time allow others the freedom to think and live differently. Ironically, it is those with the strongest beliefs who are least threatened by the differing views and lives of others and thus have the greatest capacity for tolerance. As former U.S. president John F. Kennedy described it, "tolerance implies no lack of commitment to one's own beliefs. Rather it condemns the oppression or persecution of others."

Based on that definition, tolerance seems an appropriate Christian response to those around us. As people who value freedom of belief and practices, we should condemn the oppression or persecution of others, regardless of the nature of their difference.

But we should also realize that we are as different from the person to whom we might show tolerance as they are from us, and as a result we need their tolerance in an equal measure. In this way it is analogous to charity, as considered by Uruguayan social justice activist Eduardo Galeano: "I don't believe in charity. I believe in solidarity. Charity is so vertical. It goes from the top to the bottom. Solidarity is horizontal. It respects the other person and learns from the other. I have a lot to learn from other people."

Perhaps tolerance is not something we give so much as something we need from most of the people we come into contact with. When we display the bigotry Phillip Adams admitted, we require the tolerance of those against whom we find ourselves prejudiced. Perhaps it's the best we can hope for—most of the time.

Tolerance is both necessary and good. But novelist E. M. Forster suggests that tolerance is "just a makeshift, suitable for an overcrowded and overheated planet. It carries on when love gives out, and love generally gives out as soon as we move away from our home and our friends."

But there is more. When tolerance gives out, as it does all too easily, love is again required—love for your enemies and for those whose difference has an impact upon your life. "If you love only those who love you, what good is that? . . . If you are kind only to your friends, how are you different from anyone else?" (Matt. 5:46, 47). This is love as tolerance in overdrive.

And it is the same humble love God demonstrates when "he gives his sunlight to both the evil and the good, and he sends rain on the just and on the unjust, too" (verse 45).

Attractive Girls Who Don't Smile

It was a slow afternoon as we trailed behind shoppers among the boutiques of inner-city Toronto. Assured that it was the last stop, we seated ourselves and watched the thronging customers coming and going from a certain European-inspired fashion retailer. The store drew a wealthy clientele—a quick look at a few price tags assured us of that. Couture supposedly of the highest quality and style loaded the racks, and energetic music pumped across the space, goading the mostly young women toward the cash registers. "If this was a work of art," one of our companions turned to me and commented, "I would title this *Attractive Girls Who Don't Smile.*"

It was a perceptive observation: shopping is a serious business. In fact, it has become an international pastime and definitely not a smiling matter. "We are engaged in a mania of consumption. . . . More and more people own houses that are larger and larger, and ever more crowded with stuff" (Thomas Hine, *I Want That*).

Absurdly, society as a whole, led by our governments, encourages such excess. Contemporary economies have evolved to the point where the report of consumer spending has become one of the most anticipated economic indicators. The focus on such information as vital to economic health has inverted the historical emphasis on carefulness in times of hardship or emergency. For example, in the wake of the September 11 terrorist attacks, shoppers—particularly in the U.S.—"were encouraged to think of their purchases as a blow against terrorists" *(ibid.)*. So now, we are told, we can go shopping for the good of our country—it's a patriotic act.

"Most people are able to convince themselves, at least temporarily, that it is absolutely crucial to buy items they don't really need. Indeed, our economic health depends on shoppers' ceaseless lust for the inessential" *(ibid.)*. In this regard, the primary role of advertising is to manufacture insecurity, the lurking suspicion that our lives are somehow incomplete and that the particular product promoted is just the answer to that lack.

We find ourselves taught and encouraged to chase a dangerous and self-destructive illusion. Sadly, it is a malaise from which we as Christians are not immune, and perhaps to which we are particularly susceptible. An emphasis on education, lingering echoes of the old-time Protestant work ethic, some useful teaching on stewardship, increasing denominational respectability, and many examples of God's material blessing have combined and conspired to propel us into a steady upward mobility across successive generations. With increasing wealth and position come greater opportunities for, and temptation to, further accumulation and consumption.

But one of the greatest risks for us as Christians is to assume that what we are doing is somehow inherently Christian simply because we are Christians and we are doing it. When it comes down to it, capitalism—and the rampant consumerism that drives it—is not only a Christian, but in the broader context of the economic and social inequities across the world (and even across our own societies) and the finitude of the world's resources, our consumerist capitalism may well be unchristian and perhaps even anti-Christian.

Jesus was very definite in His teaching that our lives do not consist of the things of the world around us (Matt. 6:25-32) or the "stuff" we might accumulate (Matt. 19:16-24; Luke 6:24; 12:13-21). He pointed out the danger of being distracted by "stuff" in place of the more important things of the kingdom of God (Matt. 6:19-21, 33).

Responding as Christians to the "mania of consumption" that surrounds us may not always be easy, but to minimize our participation as much as possible is a first step. Dallas Willard suggests a useful attitude: "a gentle but firm noncooperation with things that everyone knows to be wrong" *(The Divine Conspiracy)*. To buy less, to go shopping less often, to purchase carefully when we must, to get some of the "stuff" out of our lives, and to use our resources to help others are important beginnings.

Don't just buy the world's constant message that we must always be shopping!

A Theology of Tree Hugging

In 1992, 1,700 of the world's leading scientists—including 104 Nobel laureates—met to consider the state of the natural world. At the conclusion of their gathering they issued a warning: "A great change in our stewardship of the earth and the life on it is required if vast human misery is to be avoided and our global home on this planet is not to be irretrievably mutilated" ("World Scientists' Warning to Humanity," www.ucsusa.org).

While some may quibble about the edges of our looming environmental tragedies, the broadscale realities are increasingly beyond debate. Faced with the degradation of so many aspects of the natural world, it is significant that these eminent scientists—many of whom would consider themselves nonbelievers—should employ a term such as *stewardship* to describe our relationship with the world around us. It is a word that should awaken echoes of humanity's God-assigned role from Creation. Unfortunately, it's a warning that demands a change of attitude for too many Christians and Christian organizations.

For too long, many Christians have emphasized the exploitative connotations of God's charge to humanity at Creation: "Multiply and fill the earth and subdue it. Be masters over the fish and birds and all the animals" (Gen. 1:28). To many—both inside and outside Christianity—the presumed Christian attitude to the world around us is: subdue and master; use and abuse. But this ignores the more tempered and stewardly tone of the next chapter: "God placed the man in the Garden of Eden to tend and care for it" (Gen. 2:15). It's a different way of interacting with the world.

Significantly, the scientists at the special gathering called for a profound change, not just some fine adjustment. So much of how we live our lives is unsustainable, self-centered, and simply wrong. And while some of us may espouse the fashionable garb of environmental concern, most of our lives deny the reality of God's creation and our responsibilities. "Much of our contemporary creative work seems to presuppose an absurd or meaningless world, a world in which particular acts matter very little or have no larger significance. Our practices, as when we engineer or modify habitats and organisms or when we produce shoddy, cheap, and therefore wasteful products, suggest we see the universe as ours to do with as we please" (Norman Wirzba, *The Paradise of God*).

Such an attitude is profoundly anti-Christian. "The scriptural view that the whole creation belongs to God and that our role within the creation is limited, but also ennobled, to that of steward or servant seems to make little practical difference in the way many people order their lives" *(ibid.)*. Whatever attitude we may adopt or preach is worthless in the face of a contradictory manner of living.

We are enmeshed in a self-defeating and planet-destroying culture and economy. In the context of environmental degradation we encounter some big-picture issues that everyone knows to be wrong and about which we can begin to make a difference personally. "Economies built on destruction and exhaustion must be replaced with economies that model hospitality and care. We need to see that our economic lives give the most honest portrayal of how we understand salvation" *(ibid.)*.

But perhaps our first task—before we get down to the serious business of environmentalism—is to reclaim the wonder of creation. The Bible is filled with the celebration of the natural world—both by God, such as in Job 38-41, and human beings, such as Psalm 148. Jesus, too, drew from the natural world examples of

God's goodness and care (Matt. 6:26, 28-30), commending both our reliance on God and an appreciation of the simple gifts that surround us with wonder.

American agriculturalist Liberty Hyde Bailey recognized this unique relationship between a follower of Christ and the natural world when he argued that "a man cannot be a good farmer unless he is a religious man." And possibly a good farmer—or those who live with such an appropriately stewardlike attitude—is one most amenable to the religious aspect of life. "To live intimately and sympathetically with the earth is to see that we are surrounded and sustained by gifts on every side and to acknowledge that the only proper response to this unfathomable kindness is our own attention, care and gratitude" (Wirzba).

In much of the Western world we live in artificial, unsustainable, and thus unreal circumstances. We have cut ourselves off from the real world from which we draw our life. Sometimes the holiest, most profound, and most important moments in our lives are watching a sunset, feeling the rain, listening to a chorus of frogs, or even hugging a tree. Interacting with the natural world has a vital sacramental aspect as we celebrate God's abundant creativity.

As stewards of God's creation—"those who are gentle and lowly" and as such "the whole earth will belong to them" (Matt. 5:5)—we should have a preeminently global focus. We no longer need to ask, "Who is my neighbor?" (Luke 10:29), because we live with an increasing realization that we are all in this together: "There is, in practice, no such thing as autonomy. Practically speaking, there is only a distinction between responsible and irresponsible dependence" (Wirzba, quoting Wendell Barry).

We are undeniably interdependent. How we live in comparative affluence directly and indirectly influences the lives of millions of others and what happens to the limited resources of our world. As responsible stewards, we should be using the many choices in our lives, our consumer power, and our political voice to work against the blind environmental irresponsibility of much of the Western world.

When Jesus said "For God so loved the world" (John 3:16), He used the widest possible meaning of "the world." This includes all the people of the world and may well also extend to the natural world. Paul's assertion that "all creation anticipates the day when it will join God's children in glorious freedom from death and decay" (Rom. 8:21) suggests such an all-encompassing view of salvation. In light of such texts, even those who see some kind of apocalyptic sense in the destruction of our natural world must ask themselves whether God has a still bigger purpose.

Because of the prevalence of the "Christian" subdue-and-master attitude, many regard Christianity as the antithesis of environmentalism. Many intellectual circles deem Christianity as synonymous with capitalism, consumerism, Westernism, industrialism, imperialism, and even militarism. In reality, Christianity should be at the forefront of protest against such selfish and destructive attitudes and practices. As stewards of the earth, servants of all humanity, and disciples of Jesus, we must be agents of an all-embracing change in our world.

Opponents have often lampooned environmental activists as tree huggers. But if that's what we need to reforge a sense of connectedness to the natural world—and precipitate the urgent steps that will follow from a renewal of that realization—Christianity should be setting the example. Christians should be able to outhug any tree hugger. But it's not just about the tree. When we realize that the tree, the life it supports, and each of our fellow tree huggers and ourselves are all the work of an all-loving Creator, then we will rightly regard tree hugging, and all that the term has come to represent, as one of the most significant acts of our Christian experience.

Changing the World

As a longtime fan of the musical group U2, I thought one of the highlights of 2004 was the release of their *How to Dismantle an Atomic Bomb*. It is a collection of songs about life, death, love, and God, described by some reviewers as the most spiritually focused of the Irish band's 25-year career. But I was particularly struck by a passing comment in a review of the album by *Mojo* magazine: "The lifeblood of '. . . Atomic Bomb' is Bono's unstinting belief that pop stars can make a difference and that they should use their power for something above and beyond mere personal reward."

In recent years Bono has put that belief into practice in some big ways, taking on the challenges of the developing world—with a particular focus on Africa—and dealing with such issues as debt, AIDS, and fair trade. Bono *has* used his celebrity to raise the profile of these pressing humanitarian concerns.

But where does that leave us? Maybe pop stars—and some of the other rich and powerful headline makers—can change the world, but at times I begin to suspect that I will never have any impact on it.

It's not that I don't try in my own feeble ways. When I go out of my way to contact someone that I know needs encouragement, it does little to decrease the sum of suffering in the world. If I should write a letter for Amnesty International—even when a positive outcome occurs in the situation—it is still hard for me to believe that my single letter will ever make much difference. If I choose not to go to McDonald's no matter how hungry I might be, I don't think the Golden Arches money machine skips a beat. Though I might occasionally walk to work, the advertisements for bigger, faster, newer cars still continue unabated, and the oil economy still runs the world. Despite the fact that I leave my TV turned off, the ratings battles keep on. Sponsoring an orphan child in India makes no appreciable difference in world poverty levels. My letters to politicians do not seem to sway governmental policies. Forgiving someone who has hurt me does not bring peace to the Middle East. By planting a tree or a garden I am not saving a rapidly disappearing rain forest. After I refuse to regard shopping as a legitimate recreational activity, I do not see a decrease in rampant consumerism and rising household debt levels. And when I write on these kinds of real-life issues, I get only occasional support from those who would have agreed with me anyway, and criticism from those who had their minds already made up from the other perspective.

But when I am most tempted to despair, I can remind myself that each of these choices—faltering and misguided as they may be at times—is a vote for how the world should be. As a part of the kingdom of God, I am choosing to live by different rules—out of step with the world around me—with my "top priority to be part of what God is doing and to have the kind of goodness He has" (Matt. 6:33, as paraphrased in Dallas Willard's *The Divine Conspiracy*).

And there always exists the chance that somewhere along the way we just might change the world. As veteran muckraker I. F. Stone explained it: "The only kinds of fights worth fighting are those you are going to lose, because somebody has to fight them and lose and lose and lose until someday, somebody who believes as you do wins. In order for someone to win an important, major fight 100 years hence, a lot of other people have got to be willing—for the sheer fun and joy of it—to go right ahead and fight, knowing you're going to lose. You mustn't feel like a martyr. You've got to enjoy it."

An Everyday Audience

The security guard led me through the gate and onto the turf of Dairy Farmers Stadium, home of the National Rugby League's North Queensland Cowboys. I surveyed the stands encircling the playing field, feeling dwarfed in the center of the huge bowl. The manicured grass bounced beneath my feet and the lighting towers seemed to touch the night sky. I was there for a purpose and knew what I had to do. I felt a momentary thrill as I strode toward the center line.

Something about such a setting stirs the blood a little—even though the stands were empty and darkened. In the middle of the gloomy stadium a small group of people were working in preparation for an event a couple days later. They had phoned for a pizza—and I was the delivery driver. While they were pleased to see the arrival of their pizzas, it was probably not quite the same atmosphere as would have been created by 30,000 screaming fans urging me on.

It must be an incredible—and somewhat daunting experience—to live one's professional life in the packed sporting stadiums of the world. It throws into question every decision, magnifies every mistake, and causes every triumph to become an occasion for shared jubilation. For most of us, it is probably a strange mix between a dream and a nightmare. But perhaps it is not so far removed from our everyday experiences.

The Bible points out that each one of us stands center field in the stadiums that are our lives. Our audience consists of those with whom we come into daily contact: our families, our friends, our neighbors, our coworkers, and anyone else who encounters us. Most of us find our lives filled with hundreds of people each day. They are our everyday audience.

Peter urges us to "be careful how you live among your unbelieving neighbors" (1 Peter 2:12). The idea is straightforward enough: as we live upright and godly lives it will influence others as "they see what a good life you live because you belong to Christ" (1 Peter 3:16). The final part of that verse is significant. We do not just decide to be a good example or witness—it happens "because you belong to Christ." It is God working in us.

Paul echoes the same idea. He writes of a dark world filled with crooked people—so "let your lives shine brightly before them" (Phil. 2:15). But this follows his assertion that "God is working in you, giving you the desire to obey him and the power to do what pleases him" (verse 13). You fulfill your responsibility by allowing Him to manifest Himself in your life.

Leslie Williams describes ministry as "what we all do when we pitch in to help with the great festival of God on earth" *(Seduction of the Lesser Gods)*. As with any major event, the crowd adds to the atmosphere and excitement of the event itself. However, it is the players, actors, or performers who set the tone of the festivities. "This Little Light of Mine" has been sung so many times it has become a cliché, but it is actually something Jesus taught (Matt. 5:14-16). He also said we are to be the salt of the earth (verse 13), gently influencing our communities and the many lives we constantly touch.

The people around you watch how you live, how you react, how you believe, how you serve, and how you give. They want to know whether your Christianity makes any real difference in your life.

Be a Priest

Wander into the office of the academic or career adviser at your high school or college sometime and tell him or her you want to be a priest—a priest like the ones you've read about in the Old Testament. Explain that you would like to be responsible for looking after the Temple and for making judgments upon the obscure infectious diseases listed in Leviticus. While offering sacrifices sounds gory, you say, the uniform intrigues you, and most important, you would like to represent your people before God and Him to your people.

The adviser will probably pause for a moment, look puzzled, scratch his or her head for a minute or two, and begin to look for alternatives. "How about being a pastor?" he or she might suggest. But it's not really the same thing: the uniform is not as interesting, the church building probably not as impressive, and the people tend to be more independent in having their own relationship with God these days.

"But," the adviser would probably add, "you will not find many career opportunities for that kind of priest these days. No one has done those kinds of sacrifices for about 2,000 years, and, as I remember, even in those days you had to be born into the right family to become a priest. It was never something you just decided you wanted to be when you grew up—it's not like wanting to be a firefighter."

As far as career advice goes, this probably makes a lot of sense. But the Bible offers a second opinion: "You are a chosen people.

You are a kingdom of priests, God's holy nation, his very own possession" (1 Peter 2:9). All of a sudden it becomes an option again—although the costume requirements are not as strict this time, and, thankfully, the job no longer requires sheep slaughtering. However, the purpose of this new type of priesthood—which involves all believers—is much the same as that of those working in the sanctuary under Aaron's direction. "This is so you can show others the goodness of God, for he called you out of darkness into his wonderful light" (verse 9).

Being such a priest is a high and holy calling—and a great privilege. Career advisers are not necessary in this vocation. It is simply a matter of choosing to accept Jesus' sacrifice for us and becoming one of God's people. And the opportunity rests not on our efforts but on what Jesus has done for us in His death, "so let us come boldly to the throne of our gracious God. There we will receive his mercy, and we will find grace to help us when we need it" (Heb. 4:16). Learning the job means growing in relationship with God.

But to do that we must be connected with Him. That's what Jesus' story of the vine and branches was about (John 15:1-5). Again, it is a lesson we can learn from the system of worship God set up for His people at the desert sanctuary. David gives us a hint to look in that direction for guidance in Psalm 141:2. He cries to God, "Accept my prayer as incense offered to you, and my upraised hands as an evening offering."

One of the many significant features of the divinely detailed sanctuary system was the regular and cyclical nature of its services and sacrifices. The sacred blueprint calls for the burning of incense by the priests every morning and evening (Ex. 30:7, 8). Similarly, they had to perform sacrifices every day: "one in the morning and the other in the evening" (Ex. 29:39).

It was to be an ongoing relationship between God and His people—"from generation to generation" (Ex. 29:42; 30:8). And God's command also came with a promise to the people: "I will meet you and speak with you. I will meet the people of Israel there, and the Tabernacle will be sanctified by my glorious presence" (Ex. 29:42, 43).

The promise also applies to us. When we regularly seek God—in prayer, in reading His Word, in worshipping Him, in serving—we are not searching for a deity in hiding. We are looking for a God who sacrificed His own Son to rebuild the relationship with us because of His incredible love for us. The sanctuary set up by the Israelites under God's direction—in which the first priests worked—was a way of pointing people to this truth about Him: God loves us. When we choose to accept Him, we are His people, His children, and, especially, His priests to represent Him to the world around us.

Because
Life Ends

Running the Race

The annual cross-country run was a much-anticipated feature of the school calendar. For the serious athletes, it was a chance to test their training, gain recognition for their prowess, and earn a place on the school team as it moved to higher levels of competition. For the rest of us, it was an opportunity to get out of our classrooms and spend a pleasant Friday afternoon jogging or walking through the streets and parks surrounding our school. The race ranged between two and four miles (about three and six kilometers) in length (depending on the age group). Teachers lined the course, discouraging shortcuts and ensuring that the public image of the school remained intact at the end of the afternoon.

I have never been a distinguished runner, and the one year I actually tried—early on in high school—I think I finished in the top 50. In later years as the course became longer my friends and I became less motivated. In our last year we arrived at the finish line after a lap around the oval to discover the rest of the school being dismissed for the afternoon and all the teachers packing up.

Top English sports journalist Ian Stafford tells of similar experiences in his school cross-country runs. One year he and a group of friends even tried to set the record for the slowest time for the school cross-country. However, his story had one fundamental difference: in his final year of school he decided he would see how well he could do. He hatched a plan to start the race as fast as he could—at least he could say he had led the race for a part of it—and find out what would happen. As the race progressed, Stafford was unable to keep up the pace, but it took some time for any of the other competitors to catch up with him. Although some passed him, he surprised himself by finishing a creditable eighth.

Some years later, Stafford—still not a fan of running for its own sake—let a friend persuade him to enter the Lambeth Half-Marathon in south London. Not being a regular runner, he had to guess for the entry form his time for the distance. Upon arriving at the start of the race he discovered his estimated time put him among the fastest entrants, and so its staff assigned him a starting place right at the front of the 3,000 entrants.

Realizing that he had no hope of seriously competing at that level, Stafford decided to adopt the tactics from his school running "success." At the sound of the starter's gun he took off as fast as he could. Only this time the serious runners around him kept pace with him, and he soon dropped back through the field, eventually finishing around number 300.

Some months later he was amused to pick up a copy of a new book, *Fitness: Training Tips for Distance Runners.* "In one of the most blatant cases of fraud I can think of," he writes, the cover photo was of the Lambeth Half-Marathon, showing him leading the runners away from the start line.

The beginning of a race does not tell the full story. One of the joys of sport is its uncertainty. Until it is finished or the time runs out, opportunity always exists for an upset, a comeback, a last-minute play, or some other turnaround. A good start is important, but athletes must maintain focus until they have finished the race or won the game.

The Bible regularly uses the idea of running a race as a picture of living life as a Christian. It urges us to "run with endurance the race that God has set before us" (Heb. 12:1). Paul often uses this image in describing Christianity in general and his own experience: "I consider my life worth nothing to me, if only I may finish the race and complete the task the Lord Jesus has given me" (Acts 20:24, NIV).

The apostle writes with certainty of his motivation in the spiritual race. "All athletes practice strict self-control. They do it to win a prize that will fade away, but we do it for an eternal prize" (1 Cor. 9:25). For him, the manner of our running and even the ultimate result is a matter of choice. "Run in such a way that you will win," he writes (verse 24). We choose the play, and God ensures the result. Those who put their trust in Him "will run and not grow weary. They will walk and not faint" (Isa. 40:31).

The Triumph
of Death

In the prologue of Don DeLillo's epic novel *Underworld* he describes in vibrant detail the scene at the baseball game between the then New York Giants and the Brooklyn Dodgers that took place on October 3, 1951. Of particular interest to the novelist are a number of small groups of people in various sections of the crowd. One of them included then head of the FBI, J. Edgar Hoover.

The game is won at the bottom of the ninth inning by "the shot heard round the world"—a pennant-winning home run by Bobby Thomson of the Giants. The crowd is jubilant. Amid the detritus of the enthusiastic crowd a page from a magazine floats down to Hoover. It has a reproduction of a painting—*The Triumph of Death,* by sixteenth-century artist Pieter Brueghel. The lurid details of the armies of skeletons representing death marching upon the living, killing and plundering with vivid and gruesome violence, transfix the FBI director.

Hoover then looks up and across the frenzied celebrating masses. "There is something apparitional in the moment and it chills and excites him." Of course, what he recognizes in that moment is the triumph of death played out before him in the midst of that historic afternoon—the specter of death haunting our world and our individual lives.

It seems strange that death—as the antithesis of life—should be seemingly so much a part of our lives even in the midst of apparent celebrations. Yet the deaths of loved ones, of those around us, and ultimately the reality of our own death are a fundamental feature of everyone's existence.

On a global level, it is estimated that on average, about 155,000 people die every day (World Health Organization). Often we find ourselves bombarded with selected aspects of this figure—for example, that 40,000 children perish each day from malnutrition and preventable childhood diseases or that 6,500 people succumb each day from AIDS. Such preventable figures serve as markers of great tragedy, but sometimes overlooked are the thousands of "ordinary" deaths. Every day tens of thousands simply come to the end of their lives, and death is again triumphant. Even on our best days when not personally confronted by it, "death is like the rumble of distant thunder at a picnic" (W. H. Auden).

And so it is on the personal level. It is an almost unnameable terror that grips us in our most lucid and honest moments. We live, we love, we laugh, we dream, we hope, and we believe, all "in the dark valley of death." The only uncertainty is when—but eventually we will be one of those "ordinary" people who die.

Yet even in life's dark valley and almost overshadowed by our frailty and our fears, we still have the assurance of Someone who walks with us, and thus find ourselves encouraged. "Even when I walk through the dark valley of death, I will not be afraid, for you are close beside me" (Ps. 23:4).

As overwhelming as the darkness of death might appear, there is One who has conquered it, a voice that can summon us from death, a love that never leaves us. "I am convinced that nothing can ever separate us from his love. Death can't, and life can't. . . . Whether we are high above the sky or in the deepest ocean, nothing in all creation will ever be able to separate us from the love of God that is revealed in Christ Jesus our Lord" (Rom. 8:38, 39).

The stark reality is that "everyone dies. The important thing is to die well" (from the movie *Braveheart*). Perhaps the secret to dying well is paradoxically to be found in life—living in the love that promises to reach us still, even when our living is done. At times we look across our lives and our world and see the seemingly endless and exultant triumph of death. But when we recognize the love of God spilling even beyond the limits of our lives, we witness a far more powerful and infinite reality.

James Dean, Leo Tolstoy, and the Word of God

Someone once asked James Dean, the legendary Hollywood rebel, what—if anything—he respected, and his answer was "death. . . . It's the only thing left to respect. It's the one inevitable, undeniable truth. Everything else can be questioned. But death is truth. In it lies the only nobility for man and, beyond it, the only hope." Dean's untimely death in a car crash in 1955 bitterly proved his point. However, to see death as the only thing in life that we can respect and upon which one can depend is ultimately self-defeating. In the face of the inevitability of death we must search for something more.

Whatever we choose as this illusive "something more" will require a measure of faith on our behalf. The alternative offered in the Bible—as the self-proclaimed Word of God—requires such faith. It is not a mathematical formula that can lead to a precise answer, but neither does it contradict what we innately know that life is and should be. As Russian writer Leo Tolstoy once wrote: "An idea becomes close to you only when you are aware of it in your soul, when in reading about it it seems to you that it has already occurred to you, that you know it and are simply recalling it." He went on to suggest that the message presented in the Bible and particularly the teachings of Jesus in the Gospels was such an idea: it somehow seemed to fit with how he knew in his heart that he and the world generally should be.

However, in his biography of Tolstoy, A. N. Wilson, as he considered the religious zeal the Russian author exhibited in his later life, concluded that "Tolstoy's religion is ultimately the most searching criticism of Christianity which there is. He shows that it does not work" (Wilson, *Tolstoy*).

Many recognize Tolstoy as the author of *War and Peace* and *Anna Karenina,* both considered among the world's greatest novels. But in later life he dismissed them as frivolous and turned his attention to the business of living a holy life. His later writings, including *A Confession* and *Resurrection,* reflect his strivings to attain a complete and practical application of Christianity in life. Tolstoy "decided that the only way to live was the way advocated by Jesus in the Gospels: to sell all that he had and give to the poor, to take no thought for the morrow, to reject violence in all its forms, to banish revenge, to call no man Master but God alone" *(ibid.).*

However, in the process he managed to alienate his family, frustrate himself, and ultimately die in a small country railway station while on the run from his wife. While his later writings have influenced such people as Ghandi and Martin Luther King, Jr., and played a part in the survival of Christianity in Russia during the years of Communist rule (Philip Yancey, *The Jesus I Never Knew*), Tolstoy's religion still had a fatal flaw: it was not a relationship—it was a regimen.

His religion demonstrates the danger of selectively reading the Word of God and applying it to our lives. He did not accept that Jesus Christ was God, he rejected the stories of miracles recorded in the Bible, and he sought merely to live in accord with the teachings that he considered appropriate. "Tolstoy never had an encounter with Jesus, nor, as far as is recorded, did he ever believe that he had met with Jesus in prayer or had any of the mystical experiences of others who have decided that they must live as Jesus taught. Tolstoy's decision to live in this way seems to have been purely idiosyncratic and arbitrary" (Wilson).

To build an argument purporting to disprove Christianity on the basis of a form of religion without Christ is like arguing that bronchitis is a metal (as Tolstoy once did). Living in accord with a set of principles, no matter how great they might be or where they might be derived from, is quite different from entering a personal relationship with the great God of the universe. Trying to judge Christianity by anyone's life will only sell Christianity far short. And to evaluate Christianity on the basis of a Russian novelist who never had a personal relationship with God is to judge it by something that it is not.

The primary function of the Bible is to reveal God to us so that we can then enter into a relationship with Him. We could also apply Jesus' rebuke to the people of His day to Tolstoy's religion: "You search the Scriptures because you believe they give you eternal life. But the Scriptures point to me! Yet you refuse to come to me so that I can give you this eternal life" (John 5:39, 40).

In Jesus, God made the effort to bridge the gap between deity and the human race in the hope that He could establish a closer connection between Him and us. The Lord did not call us simply to live in accord with the teachings of Jesus—or any other portion of the Bible that we might arbitrarily choose—but rather to become sons and daughters of God. It was for this purpose that "the Word became human and lived here on earth among us" (John 1:14).

So we find ourselves left with an all-or-nothing kind of choice. For the Word of God to be of real benefit to us, we must accept the Bible as God revealed to humanity in a written form. To an extent it is similar to accepting Jesus as God displayed to humanity in a form "made flesh." Once we arrive at this belief, we will then regard Scripture as the infallible revelation of God's will. The Bible will constitute our rule of faith: the standard of character, the test of experience, the authoritative revealer of doctrines, and the trustworthy record of God's acts in history.

Only then can we be assured that we will not be disappointed as we embrace the Bible as the Word of God in its blessed completeness. In a world in which everything is fleeting, the Word of God and the knowledge of God revealed through it will provide an unshakable foundation for both our future hope and our present Christian lives.

The Bible assures us a number of times of the permanence and eternal reliability of the Word of God: "The grass withers, and the flowers fade, but the word of our God stands forever" (Isa. 40:8; cf. 1 Peter 1:24, 25; Matt. 5:18). "People are like the grass that fades away" (Isa. 40:6; cf. 1 Peter 1:24), a fact recognized by James Dean. Part of our everyday lives, this reality should spark our quest for "something more" that only the Bible can give us.

In the face of our undeniable mortality we find hope. When confronted with the questions life and death put to us—even the very question raised by James Dean—we can borrow the words of his answer.

What—if anything—can we respect? The Word of God. It's the only thing left—the one inevitable, undeniable truth. Everything else can be questioned. But the Word of God is truth. In it lies the only nobility for humanity and, beyond it, the only hope.

"Hell Is for Other People"

Surveys of belief often come up with interesting anomalies. For example, a recent study by the Barna Research Group compared Americans' understandings of the afterlife (www.barna.org). The results reveal a snapshot of both the state of belief and of human nature.

As a starting point, 81 percent of those surveyed believe in some kind of afterlife. Seventy-six percent support the concept of a heaven, leaving 5 percent who hold to a less-than-conventional postexistence existence. Notably, a belief in hell is less popular than heaven, being endorsed by only 71 percent of respondents.

Contrary to the traditional concept of hell, in this survey more people regarded it as a "state of eternal separation from God's presence" (39 percent) than those describing it as "an actual place of suffering and torment" (32 percent).

However, things get particularly interesting when the survey asked participants where they expected to end up after death. Twenty-four percent were honest enough to admit they have "no idea." Sixty-four percent claimed to be heaven-bound. But perhaps the most attention-grabbing statistic is the just 1 percent who assumed that they would end up in hell. The bottom line according to the Barna report: a widely held concept that "hell is for other people."

Speculating on what percentages of humanity might be saved or lost is futile and perhaps dangerous. But even if—by virtue of the overflowing grace of God—those whose end is hell might be as low as 1 percent, the only relevant percentages are 100 or zero. It's an all-or-nothing question for each of us.

Calvinist minister Jonathan Edwards presented one of history's most famous—or infamous—sermons on July 8, 1741. Edwards was one of the most powerful preachers in a revival known as the Great Awakening in the New England region of the United State during the 1740s. Although he reportedly had only a feeble voice, one of his biographers described his preaching as "a kind of moral inquisition" in which "sinners were put upon argumentative racks, and beneath screws" (William Safire, *Lend Me Your Ears*).

While we have arguments with some of Edwards' theology, the sermon—"Sinners in the Hands of an Angry God"—paints a graphic and sobering picture of the risk at which all of us stand if we choose to live apart from the grace of God. He depicts the sinner as a spider hanging by a single thread above a pit of destruction with "nothing to lay hold of to save yourself, nothing to keep off the flames of wrath, nothing of your own, nothing that you have ever done, nothing that you can do."

It is uncomfortable stuff. However, while it is much more popular to talk of God's love, the Bible does present an alternative to the "happily ever after" ending that we like to dwell upon. Life without God has an unhappy and unpleasant end: an "outer darkness, where there will be weeping and gnashing of teeth" (Matt. 25:30). It is the bit about "perishing" that John 3:16 tells us we can avoid if we want to.

Ultimate destruction also provides an added urgency for our witnessing. While our primary motivation for sharing our faith with others might be God's love for them, our concern for others—especially people we care about—can also reflect a realization of the alternate reality. We have both eternal life to gain and eternal death to avoid.

Some of the greatest evangelists throughout history have found themselves driven by a sense of possible eternal loss. C. T. Studd, missionary to China, reputedly once stated that his mission was to set up a "rescue shop within a yard of hell."

This is the point at which whatever we might be choosing—or not choosing—about our connection with God becomes deadly serious. That is why we need a Savior as well as why we need to share Him and His love with those around us.

Death Unnatural

During the past few years a band on the popular music scene went by the unlikely name N.E.R.D.—an acronym for No One Ever Really Dies. The name suggests one of the most common beliefs about what lies beyond the present. The popular conception suggests that death is simply a stage through which we pass in our eternal existence. This might mean going straight to heaven (or hell), reincarnation, or some similar altered state of existence. Life is a continuum, with death as a natural part of that—or so it is argued. And again we hear the echo of the beguiling but doomed offer of immortality: "You won't die. . . . You will become just like God" (Gen. 3:4, 5).

Such a belief brings with it serious consequences for other things that we must take into account or otherwise explain. For example, the dead inhabiting some form of spirit world; the possibility of the living making contact with such beings; the potential for the dead to effect revenge upon those who may have wronged them in life; and the heartache of the dead watching loved ones experience tragedy and loneliness in this life.

It is a concept with significant ideological—and biblical—difficulties: "To believe in the immortality of the soul is to believe that though John Brown's body lies a-moldering in the grave, his soul goes marching on simply because marching on is the nature of souls just the way producing butterflies is the nature of caterpillars. . . . True or false, this is not the biblical view, although many who ought to know better assume it is" (Frederick Buechner, *Wishful Thinking*).

But perhaps the most serious of the many problems connected with such a belief is not a philosophical or theological difficulty. It's a more practical consideration: the natural abhorrence we have of death. Despite attempts by various philosophical systems to present it as "normal," "natural," or even something better, this belief quickly collapses when we experience grief. Death is always a tragedy and is regarded as such by those who have "lost" a family member or friend. That is why we, as a society, spend so much on health, on fitness, on suicide prevention strategies, on drug rehabilitation, and on other programs or regimens aimed to extend our existence, even in the face of terrible disappointments and tragedies.

Such behavior flies in the face of our attempts at spiritualizing and philosophizing human tragedy. As Buechner goes on to suggest, "one of the blunders religious people are particularly fond of making is the attempt to be more spiritual than God" *(ibid.)*. And we can see His attitude to death played out in the life of Jesus. For Jesus, death was not a blessed, spiritual progression. When confronted with those mourning the dead, He did not try to comfort them with a discourse on death as a part of the natural order of things. Instead, He stopped the mourning and gave them reason to rejoice—but not before, at least in the story of Lazarus, Jesus shared for a moment their sorrow. The shortest but perhaps most profound of Bible verses is "Jesus wept" (John 11:35).

We observe similar reluctance as He approached His own death. As evidenced by His anguished prayers in Gethsemane, Jesus obviously did not appreciate the naturalness of death, even though it was an end He had anticipated for some time. Indeed His heroism, as presented throughout the New Testament, was in overcoming death—"death is swallowed up in victory" (1 Cor. 15:54)—not its acceptance as something good.

For the Christian, death is not a natural part of life. It is the enemy—but a defeated one. Death is a tragedy, but, because of Jesus, even in the face of such tragedy we have hope.

It Can't Rain
All the Time . . .

T*he Crow*, starring the late Brandon Lee and directed by Alex Proyas, was a big hit on movie screens across the world some years ago and now enjoys something of a "cult classic" status in video release. It is a story of violent revenge, situated in a city of rain-soaked nights. However, one particular scene in this otherwise bleak movie epitomizes hope even in darkness.

A young girl sits on the edge of the city footpath with her feet in the gutter as rain continues to fall around her in the gloom of the city night. She is one of the victims of the story—a young girl, left alone in a hostile city, with nowhere to turn and no prospects for anything more than the desolation and isolation that she is already experiencing. Behind her, observed by the camera, a dark figure approaches and gently states that "it can't rain all the time." She turns quickly and immediately recognizes her friend. Amid the darkness and the rain there exists a glimmer of hope: a promise of ultimate and inevitable redemption.

In the world in which we find ourselves, in the problems and difficulties in our own lives, and in the broader tragedies of our society and world, the darkness and the rain often discourage us. However, regardless of our circumstances, regardless of how bad the world around may appear or even actually be, we can have a complete hope in an ultimate and inevitable redemption.

Such a hope fills the Bible. Jesus, fully aware that our lives in this world would often feel hopeless, gave His disciples—and us—a command and a promise: "Don't be troubled. You trust God, now trust in me. . . . When everything is ready, I will come and get you, so that you will always be with me where I am" (John 14:1-3). Because of the certainty that we can have in God's goodness and trustworthiness, it is a promise upon which we can rely.

Paul, the first and greatest Christian missionary, often faced hardships, opposition, and difficulties. He recognized the darkness of the world in which he lived and died. It was a world that he did not understand—"Now we see but a poor reflection as in a mirror" (1 Cor. 13:12, NIV)—but Paul had a faith that the promises of God would allow him one day to see fully—"then we shall see face to face" (verse 12, NIV).

Throughout his writings the apostle considers that what God has done for us in sending Jesus to die for us acts as a guarantee of the great ultimate redemption to come. He uses the ideas of a deposit and an engagement as reflecting the certainty that we can currently enjoy in a present relationship with God—"as a guarantee he has given his Holy Spirit" (2 Cor. 5:5).

Paul rejoiced in the hope of the Lord's final victory on this earth and in the return of Jesus. In 1 Thessalonians 4 he begins his description of this glorious event with "according to the Lord's own word" (verse 15, NIV) and concludes with the assertion: "And so we will be with the Lord forever" (verse 17, NIV). It is only the absolute certainty of this hope that would allow Paul to say, as he considered the sufferings of his life—stonings, beatings, imprisonment, shipwrecks, riots, and finally an impending execution—"Yet what we suffer now is nothing compared to the glory he will give us later" (Rom. 8:18).

No matter how good our circumstances might be, we can all readily find things in our lives and in our world that we would like improved. The good news is that, no matter how bad our circumstances might be, we can share Paul's certainty in this ultimate and inevitable redemption. "If we do not believe that, then, as the apostle Paul noted in 1 Corinthians 15, there's not much reason for being a Christian in the first place. And if we do believe this, it should change our lives" (Philip Yancey, "Whatever Happened to Heaven?" in *I Was Just Wondering*).

The Finch

For a short period of time my wife was licensed to care for wildlife, and we nursed a succession of young, abandoned, and injured birds back to good health—or they met a sadder end. But one little bird stayed much longer.

The small finch had fallen out of its nest and did not have proper feathers when it arrived at our house. In the following days, as I attempted to feed the bird I became frustrated with trying to place food in its mouth—so I sat it on my finger. Thus began the process of its taking over our house.

For the next six months "Finchie"—the bird never really received a proper name—had the free run of our house. Although it slept in a corner on a high shelf, it also liked the warmth and noise atop the computer monitor. Finchie would fly to greet us on our return home, would respond to our whistling, and would ride on our heads and shoulders as we went around the house. At mealtime it would vigorously attack whatever was on our plates or forks, and the creature seemed to have a sometimes-dangerous fascination with mouths and teeth.

It seemed almost impossible to believe so much personality could be packed into such a tiny bird. And Finchie soon found a significant place in our lives.

But one day I stepped out our front door to the mailbox. To my horror, I felt a tiny push-off from the back of my shoulder and turned to see the tiny bird disappear into some nearby trees. The finch was gone.

Although we called and whistled, we received no response. We prayed. And we even called the local radio station—but they tried to conceal their amusement at the prospect of listing a missing finch among their usual round of lost dogs and cats. It was a sad day. Possibly we even asked God why it had to happen that way. Why was it so difficult for this tiny source of joy to be content to remain in our home?

But somehow it reminded me of the story at the end of the book of Jonah. God caused a plant to grow, giving the prophet shade from the hot Mesopotamian sun. "This eased some of [Jonah's] discomfort, and Jonah was very grateful for the plant" (Jonah 4:6). But then the plant died, and the prophet was mad at God. The Lord responded to his feelings: "You feel sorry about the plant, though you did nothing to put it there" (verse 10).

Somehow the incident resonated with our experience. While an ending brings sadness, perhaps a better attitude would be to celebrate what has been. Rather than yielding to the misery of an ending, gratitude for the absolute grace the finch brought to us would have been more appropriate. The life and personality of that little bird had come to us unearned, even unexpected. Perhaps it was a glimpse of how the world should be—but even that glimpse itself came as a gift.

Charles Dickens suggested that life is a constant series of partings. And there is a certain poignancy to his observation. But it ignores the fact that for every parting, there first has to be a meeting; and for every ending, there was a beginning. The beginnings often go unheralded—even unsought—but they are no less real. We recognize the significance of beginnings only in retrospect and so can easily miss them. And the best are those that rejoice in everything that happened before the ending—even in the midst of sorrow.

While it may be difficult to apply the lesson of the finch next time we are at the funeral of a loved one or suffer some other tragedy or disappointment, perhaps by faith we can begin to catch something of this attitude. After all, the Bible assures that at the end there will be at least one more beginning than there have been endings—and that many of the endings will be found to have been only a milestone in an eternal beginning (Rev. 21:1-5). And with God the beginnings last forever.

Because Life
Begins Again

Once Upon a Time . . .

"O nce upon a time . . . "—the phrase signals the beginning of some of our best-known and best-loved stories. From storytellers and storybooks throughout history—and more recently in movie adaptations—such "once upon a time" narratives have brought generations of audiences and readers to the point where "they all lived happily ever after."

Often people have simplified and dismissed them as children's stories, something we might be expected to grow out of. But to treat them in this way risks missing some of their profound significance. C. S. Lewis spoke of a possible higher reality behind such stories when he described the myths and stories passed down through history as "a real though unfocused gleam of divine truth falling on human imagination" *(Miracles)*. Such stories let us see human life from a cosmic perspective.

While they present this divine truth with varying degrees of accuracy, the real resonance of these stories occurs in similar elements recognizable in the gospel story—the central story and claims of Christianity. Reading the Bible as a true "fairy tale" can bring a new appreciation to the history of God and humanity that we find there.

The Bible begins with the "once upon a time" equivalent—"In the beginning . . . " (Gen. 1:1)—and reaches a similar ending— "And they [God's people] will reign forever and ever" (Rev. 22:5).

All the other Bible stories are the tragedies, disappointments, high-lights, and hopes between that perfect beginning and perfect end. Put simply, the Bible is the history of the journey between those two points. It gives us a cosmic viewpoint, a divinely ordained glimpse of a greater reality than can be seen just through human eyes.

J.R.R. Tolkien—the master of modern fairy tales and a Christian—invented the term *eucatastrophe* for the turn of events in such a story that produces a happy ending and that makes everything "live happily ever after" despite the sadness and evil that have gone before. In an essay titled "On Fairy-Stories," Tolkien concluded that "the Gospels contain a fairy-story, or a story of a larger kind which embraces all the essence of fairy-stories." In the stories of Jesus, he argues, we find "the greatest and most complete conceivable 'eu-catastrophe.' . . . The Birth of Christ is the 'eucatastrophe' of Man's history. The Resurrection is the 'eucatastrophe' of the story of the Incarnation. The story begins and ends in joy" (in *Tree and Leaf*).

Thus the temptation for those choosing to reject the stories and claims of Christianity as presented in the Bible would be to argue that such a correlation with tales and legends is evidence of the ele-ment of wishful thinking in Christian belief. According to such an argument, the similarities between Christianity and tales point to the fictional nature of the Christian story.

However, Jesus' disciples anticipated—or at least responded to—such an allegation. "For we are not making up clever stories when we told you about the power of our Lord Jesus Christ and his com-ing again. We have seen his majestic splendor with our own eyes" (2 Peter 1:16). While we might find fairy-tale elements in the Christian story, there is one significant difference: in Jesus the tale, the glimpse of that hoped-for greater reality, became history—and that was the real and personal experience of His earliest followers.

Yet this historical reality does not diminish the mythic elements—the cosmic viewpoint—of this greatest of stories. "Myth, in becoming Fact, does not cease to be Myth; just as [in Jesus] God, in becoming Man, does not cease to be God" (C. S. Lewis, *God in the Dock*).

So the other aspect of the similarities between the Bible and legends, hinted at by Lewis, is that such tales point to a greater reality—one that in the history of our world has seen its most complete expression in Jesus Christ. Rather than a story too good to be true, the gospel is a story that is "too good not to be true" (Frederick Buechner, *Telling the Truth*).

And it is a story in which we have a part. By choosing to follow the God of this ultimate tale, we can choose to live "happily ever after."

The Longing
for Home

My former hometown—Townsville, north Queensland, Australia—is one of those communities it always feels nice to come home to. Approaching it from the south, you round a corner in the highway and find yourself at the top of a small hill—and the town spreads out on the distant plain before you. It's one of those homecoming scenes in which the music swells and you know the credits are about to roll.

Of course, a local radio station has employed the position as the site for a billboard, welcoming motorists and urging them to adjust their car radios to its channel. Experiencing this "homecoming" on one occasion after being six months away and reflecting on the various "homes away from home" that we had been privileged to be a part of around the world got me thinking what "home" might mean in our lives.

"Home" carries a variety of meanings. But for most of us, it represents a collection of places and people that hold a significant place in our hearts.

The people are vital—but many of them eventually move on and become just memories. The places are significant—rounding that bend just out of Townsville would mean much less to those who call Cairns home and still have four hours' driving ahead of them—but it is something more than a geographical location. As Bob Dylan has commented, "I never was a kid who could go home.

I never had a home which I could just take a bus to." It is a statement that many of us—particularly those who have moved around a number of times in our lives—could identify with.

Perhaps more important than a place is the feeling of being "at home." Maybe it's what we are suggesting when we invite guests to "make themselves at home." And given the right conditions, it does not take much to begin to feel at home: you get used to the feel of the house or room in which you live; you begin to find your way around nearby streets; you see some of the same people on the streets and in their gardens; and you learn where things are on the shelves in your closest supermarket or corner store. Soon, it is familiar—there is a growing feeling of "home," a certain sense of security.

But just as quickly the feeling can vanish. You come home to find your house burglarized—and it does not feel quite so safe anymore. The sense of security shatters, and it takes time to rebuild it. We realize how tenuous our "at home" feelings really are.

It is also true on a larger scale. A plane gets flown into a building, a bomb explodes in a crowded area, or other acts of violence happen to destroy our sense of security. We find ourselves unemployed, a friend or relative is diagnosed with a frightening disease, or we begin to feel the slow creep of old age—and suddenly we don't feel quite so "at home" anymore. Such things remind us of our innate longing for home—or "at-home-ness."

In a way we are always homesick. We are never more than foreigners and nomads here on earth. "And obviously people who talk like that are looking forward to a country they can call their own. . . . They [are] looking for a better place, a heavenly homeland" (Heb. 11:14-16).

Not surprisingly, our longing for "home"—for the security of being "at home"—finds its full answer only beyond this world. The titles to the last four chapters of Frederick Buechner's *The Longing for Home* summarize the components of this "at home" feeling: "Faith." "Hope." "Grace." "Jesus."

Perhaps our deepest longing for home involves our desire for God. In response to that longing, God provides both the home and the way.

At the End
of the World

The sun beat down upon us, its heat radiating up from the blacktop of the basketball court. Yet for some reason that I cannot recall we were still playing—and sweating.

Bushfires burned out of control in the hills to the west of the city, and their smoke blanketed the suburbs, adding to the oppressiveness of the afternoon. We played only sporadically. Each renewed game would soon lose its energy, and we would all stick our heads under a nearby tap—splashing water on those waiting—and shelter in small patches of shade at the side of the court.

Talking languidly, we watched the heat haze shimmer over the basketball court. Usually one or two people would continue shooting, until, after a few minutes, the rest of us returned to the court, and another game broke out.

Late in the afternoon the sun began to descend through the layer of haze on the western horizon, turning a blood red through the smoke. We had reached another pause—they were becoming more frequent—and the dramatic sunset caught our attention.

Our conversation was subdued, but, as we went back to the game, one of the players commented, "I never expected to be playing basketball at the end of the world."

We paused again for a moment, surveying the apocalyptic sunset, before continuing the game.

It was a throwaway line, but the momentary pause on that

sweat-soaked afternoon spoke of a shared consciousness of the possibilities of the end of the world and the question as to what might be an appropriate activity for such a time.

No matter what our beliefs, we seem intrigued by the whole concept of the end of the world. The fascination does not usually last long, however, and we often quickly resume whatever game the thought might have interrupted. But the truth is that in our ordinary, everyday circumstances we are always at the end of the world—and it is quite likely we will meet our end and/or the end of the world somewhere doing something that we would not have expected.

In J.R.R. Tolkien's *The Hobbit* travelers visit a town in which ancient legends tell of a day to come when "gold would flow in the rivers . . . and all that land would be filled with new song and new laughter." The old songs of the townspeople recorded the stories. "But this pleasant legend did not much affect their daily business."

Our consciousness of a conclusion to this world and then of another world to come, both on a global scale and individually, can too easily become the stuff of "pleasant"—or frightening—"legend." The Bible assures us not only that our world will end but that this certainty must make a difference in our lives.

It is not a matter of fear but of priorities—and so much of the "stuff" that distracts us is nowhere near as important as considering what we might be doing at the end of the world.

A Nike advertising campaign of recent years raised the question—through images of various athletes pushing themselves to their absolute limits—"What are you getting ready for?" The obvious answer is that what you are doing right now determines that for which you will be ready.

No matter how near or distant the end of the world might be, the basis of the future is always now. Now is when we must make choices as to what God really means to us and, as a result, how we will live our lives. Peter wrote to Christians urging that, as the end of the world is near, they should "love each other deeply" and live in such a way "that in all things God may be praised" (1 Peter 4:8, 11, NIV).

It is a matter of priorities, a question of what you are getting ready for.

Celebrating Persecution?

For many of us—at least in the Western world—mention of persecution raises images of early Christians' encounters with lions as a form of public entertainment or medieval martyrs singing hymns while burning at the stake. Or perhaps if of a more prophetic bent we might look forward with a grim fascination to a "time of trouble" in which another generation will have opportunity to display such self-sacrificing commitment. As such, we might recognize a heritage and a future challenge while largely ignoring the world in which we now live.

From time to time we read accounts of Christian missionaries killed, pastors beaten, church members jailed, and church buildings burned—but they are usually in places we cannot pronounce and that we certainly could not find on a map. Yet they represent glimpses of a somber reality. In much of the world and through most of Christian history, being a Christian has been dangerous.

An estimated 160,000 Christians die for their faith around the world each year (The Voice of the Martyrs, www.persecution.com). Their stories are not merely the stuff of dusty history textbooks or prophetic expectation. They are the life-and-death experiences of many in the world today.

But perhaps we should not be surprised by the presence of persecution. Jesus warned His disciples, "Don't imagine that I came to bring peace to the earth! No, I came to bring a sword" (Matt.

10:34). He goes on to portray the discord and hatred—even within families—that would result from following Him.

At first glance, the apparent dissonance between this assertion and statements such as "blessed are the peacemakers" (Matt. 5:9, NIV) might jolt us. And it seems a long way from the angel choirs proclaiming "peace on earth to all whom God favors" (Luke 2:14). However, in His warning to His disciples, Jesus was not setting out a goal of His ministry. Instead, He was talking about the tough reality of living in a world largely hostile to radical, transforming Christianity: "In these words, then, Jesus was warning His followers that their allegiance to Him might cause conflict. . . . It is well that they should be forewarned, for then they could not say, 'We never expected that we should have to pay this price for following Him!'" (F. F. Bruce, *The Hard Sayings of Jesus*).

It is a forewarning that has slipped down the back of the sofa for most of Western Christianity. We do not laminate such statements in attractive wall plaques, superimposing them on cute photos of kittens, or inscribe them with a flourish on Christian greeting cards.

In an American literature class in the university English department in which I once worked, students received an exam question exploring aspects of redemption in Nathaniel Hawthorne's *Scarlet Letter*. Despite the depth of Puritan thought underlying this book, not one student mentioned the possibility of redemption found through suffering. Such attitudes reflect a significant shift in our society's view of life and its purpose.

Our age of overabundance constantly assures us that we can obtain the answers to all our needs, wants, and pain with little more than a credit card. The mythmakers of corporate marketing ceaselessly prompt us toward image, ease, and effortless push-button living. Even some within Christian marketing and publishing urge us to look for ever-increasing evidence of God's blessing, usually in the material and physical. We certainly do not live in a society that considers suffering a virtue.

But Jesus said, "God blesses you when you are mocked and persecuted and lied about because you are my followers. Be happy about it! Be very glad!" (Matt. 5:11, 12). It may require much work to rebuild an attitude of appreciation of suffering as a part of our Christian experience. Perhaps in the absence of direct threat of persecution we could begin with a radical focus on God's kingdom with its promise of a "great reward" beyond this world.

It will prepare us to endure the brutality of religious persecution, the barbs of mockery, and the pain of betrayal. Jesus' beatitude applies not only to situations of violent death, cruel torture, and ugly taunts but also to the more everyday realities of social isolation, job loss, division in families, and office jokes. From the greatest atrocities to the smaller but nonetheless still significant everyday challenges to our Christian commitment, this beatitude reminds us of God's blessing and enjoins us to rejoicing.

Yet it is certainly not an automatic human reaction. C. S. Lewis admits the extreme difficulty of reaching the beatitude's attitude to suffering: "I suppose that if one loves a person enough one would actually wish to share every part of his life; and I suppose the great saints thus really *want* to share the divine sufferings and that is how they actually desire pain. But this is far beyond me. To grin and bear it and (in some feeble, desperate way) to trust is the utmost most of us can manage" *(Letters to an American Lady)*.

To "grin and bear it" might well be an admirable human response to persecution and suffering, yet the beatitude urges us to "be happy about it!"—and not just despite our persecution but *because* of it. In the context of the Beatitudes as a whole—many of which urge us to be meek, peacemakers, and the like—one might even be tempted (perhaps if it did not hurt so much) to seek out persecution.

In practical terms, this is probably not the course of greatest wisdom. Jesus instructed His disciples to flee the destruction of Jerusalem (Matt. 24:16), and we find many examples of God's intervention to rescue His followers from martyrdom, persecution, and other harm. In short, "there is no wisdom or virtue in seeking unnecessary martyrdom or deliberately courting persecution; yet it is, none the less, the persecuted or martyred Christian in whom the pattern of the Master is most unambiguously realized" (C. S. Lewis, *The Four Loves*).

Instead of urging us to invite or seek persecution, the concluding verses of the Beatitudes call for us to rejoice in the higher purpose of living as a pilgrim in this world, of living as part of a larger, transcendent kingdom. Such a life may well have ugly results in an ugly world. That is why "the ancient prophets were persecuted too" as citizens of the kingdom of heaven, because "they were too good for this world" (Heb. 11:38).

Probably the Bible's best example of this attitude is Paul's letter to the Philippians. Written from prison in Rome around A.D. 61, Philippians is a model of rejoicing in the midst of persecution. The apostle assures his readers of his joy at the progress of God's work in our world. "I rejoice. And I will continue to rejoice" (Phil. 1:18).

The kingdom of God as described in the Beatitudes and more broadly in the Sermon on the Mount provides a superhuman way of seeing the world—a glimpse of God's viewpoint. A confrontation with the realities of this divine kingdom will profoundly alter our values, our priorities, our actions, our relationships, and our self-image. It will also shake up our attitudes to personal security and social acceptance.

When we realize the "great reward" that is membership in the kingdom of God, we can echo Paul no matter what life or this world throws at us: "For I live in eager anticipation and hope . . . that I will always be bold for Christ, as I have been in the past, and that my life will always honor Christ, whether I live or I die" (verse 20).

TEOTWAWKI

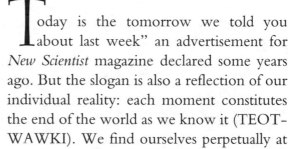

Today is the tomorrow we told you about last week" an advertisement for *New Scientist* magazine declared some years ago. But the slogan is also a reflection of our individual reality: each moment constitutes the end of the world as we know it (TEOTWAWKI). We find ourselves perpetually at the end of known life and the beginning of the unknown. Whether we approach it in irrational fear or unfounded hope, the weight of the future is a futile burden. In *The Screwtape Letters* the devils want humanity "haunted by visions of an imminent heaven or hell upon earth . . . a whole race perpetually in pursuit of the rainbow's end, never honest, nor kind, nor happy *now*" (C. S. Lewis). It is their evil desire that we will constantly sacrifice the present to the future possibility of pleasure or horror.

We live in a world shadowed by the perpetual possibility of its own end. Umberto Eco portrayed this in his *The Name of the Rose,* a story set in the fourteenth century. In the light of continuing floods and famines the preachers announced the end of the world but the "parents and grandparents remembered the same story in the past as well, so they came to the conclusion that the world was always about to end." And in a sense that's a reasonable conclusion. The Bible presents many of its prophecies in ways that are continually applicable. Even God depicts Himself as transcending the strictures of time: "'I am the Alpha and the Omega—the beginning and the end,' says the Lord God. 'I am the one who is, who always was, and who is still to come, the Almighty One'" (Rev. 1:8).

It is a challenge for us as mere humans—bound by our limitations of time and space—even to begin to understand a God so vast. But if we somehow grasp a tiny fragment of this perspective, then perhaps TEOTWAWKI is relatively unimportant. The eternity of our God is far more significant than the end of our speck of a world.

Yet so often we seem to get this the wrong way around. Life continually bombards us with TEOTWAWKI theories and stories. People invent their own version of the future, usually much more interesting than the mundane present. And this imagined future can provide excuse or reason for all manner of activity or inactivity.

It is possible we have the wrong perspective when we continually look for or expect an end to our world. Perhaps we should view it in a different way. Maybe we should think of it as the real history of our world is yet to begin. C. S. Lewis quotes poet John Donne in suggesting that our present lives are perhaps best regarded as "tuning our instruments. The tuning up of the orchestra can be itself delightful, but only to those who can, in some measure, however little, anticipate the symphony" (in *Reflections on the Psalms*). When we look at life this way, the orchestra is yet to explode into a glorious overture signaling the symphony of real life, one far beyond our current limitations and disappointments.

The future belongs to God. When we belong to Him TEOTWAWKI is just another part of our journey with Him: "Our fears for today, our worries about tomorrow, and even the powers of hell can't keep God's love away" (Rom. 8:38). Because of this eternal fact—as the musical group REM put it—"It's the end of the world as we know it . . . and I feel fine."

Off the Chart

We like to be right, to have it all fig-
ured out with all the answers. So it
is probably natural enough in a church focused on the future always to be trying to
have all the details nailed down. In the past
we frequently developed prophecy charts
detailing events extending from the past to
the future and setting out supposed end-time timetables. The as-
sumption is that if we can learn the sequences, we will then be able
to identify our current prophetic location on the time line, find
where current world events are on that continuum, and thereby en-
ergize ourselves for renewed apocalyptic expectancy.

A knowledge of Bible prophecy has its points—why would God
have put it in the Bible otherwise?—and there is value in an awareness of current issues in our world. But a preoccupation with
prophetic time-lining has risks.

The first is that of developing an arrogant and unbalanced faith:
"As a movement within Christianity that is acutely conscious of its
distinctiveness and so regards itself as a 'prophetic movement,' we
are tempted to make this distinctiveness our theological and spiritual
center and thus to become theologically and spiritually eccentric.
This temptation should be consciously, conscientiously, and constantly resisted" (Fritz Guy, *Thinking Theologically*).

We can have all the right answers about Bible prophecy and still
miss God and who He wants us to be. Jesus said, "You must love
the Lord your God" and "Love your neighbor as yourself" (Matt.

22:37, 39). Of course, a love for God will motivate us to know the things of God and to share them with our neighbors because of our love for God and our love for them. But if, on the great and glorious day when our God returns with untold power and splendor to take us home to live with Him in glory forever, our first reaction is a self-righteous and self-satisfied "I told you so" to the unbelievers shaking in terror around us, it is quite possible we will not only have missed the point but also the trip home.

A second shortcoming of a prophecy-chart faith is that it tends to focus our thinking on this world and the events leading up to the Second Coming. While this is probably natural enough, it is not the ultimate aim. Such charts lay out the events of our world in detail, but when they reach the point of the Second Coming, they all become a little vague. Yet what comes afterward is the main point—we will spend eternity in that period the charts have little to say about.

Just contemplate for a moment Revelation 22:5: "The Lord God will shine on them. And they [we] will reign forever and ever." The enormity of that statement is mind-boggling. Because of our limited point of view, perhaps we will have to live forever before we can begin to sense its vastness. The Bible is vague on the experience of heaven, mostly because we will always struggle to express the infinite in finite language.

The images given in the Bible are attempts to express the sublime in the culture in which humanity first received it, making it all the more difficult for those of us further removed from those times. And we have seen too many clichés of floating on clouds to be able to grasp the reality of heaven. Some of the best Bible pictures we have of heaven are the lists of bad things that will *not* be there (Isa. 65:20-25; Rev. 21:3, 4). Scripture assures us of "new heavens and a new earth—so wonderful that no one will even think about the old ones anymore" (Isa. 65:17).

We have cheapened the concept of heaven. Advertising uses it for such things as ice cream, bedding, holidays, and other things as metaphors of good things. Even in our churches, we encourage younger people to focus on what kind of pet animal they want to have in heaven. While such things point us to something vaguely good—it still falls short of the best. So we are left with "guesses, only guesses. And if they are not true something better will be" (C. S. Lewis, *Letters to Malcolm: Chiefly on Prayer*).

And missing that something better is the greatest risk of prophetic distraction. These charts easily twist everything into a story about ourselves instead of a story about God. It is only because of what He has done for us that we have any hope at the end of our world. It is only because of what God will do for us that there is a purpose. And it is only because of who He is that Scripture gives us a glimpse of things to come, that we receive a minor role to play in His big plan for the universe, and that we matter at all. Any "right" answers we have are just another of His gifts.

The Eternal
Moment of Joy

 T he sky will not always be empty. Its blue expanse will not always stare back vacantly in response to our urgent and desperate prayers. Eventually "despair dies into infinite hope" (George MacDonald, *Phantastes*), and there will come a day . . .

In that moment your eyes will meet those of Jesus—and you will realize you have always known Him. That this is what you have been looking for all your life. The ultimate spiritual experience, this is knowing and loving God truly, completely, and eternally. It is the purpose for which He created you.

Imagine one of those occasions when you have shared an exciting secret in a telephone conversation earlier in the day. Only you and that other person know about it. Later in the day you are in a crowd of other people when that individual arrives. You are busy with other people—maybe a meeting is in progress—but your eyes meet for just an instant as the other person enters the room. Since you cannot talk at the moment, you plan to meet with your friend as soon as the meeting is over. But in that instant a flash of recognition takes place between both of you. You smile—the connection is made, and you will have plenty of time to talk later.

After Jesus returns you have eternity to catch up with Him. Your eyes meet for just an instant amid the glorious and awesome uproar accompanying His return to this world. Both terrified and elated, you want to fall down and worship. At the same time, you want to shout and sing and dance. And all of a sudden you can fly. But the central moment is that instant in which your eyes met—God and you, face to face. Unspeakable joy surges through you.

Throughout life you have experienced many little tastes of such joy. All of us have had occasions during which something beyond us has not only drawn us out of ourselves but called us to something more. Perhaps they have been experiences of pilgrimage, devotion, or worship. We have received glimpses of something unknown and unknowable overarching our lives and the universe as a whole. At times God has seemed particularly close—as if you could almost touch Him. Now all those moments rush together in that one connection, that simple look: "that central music in every pure experience which [has] always just evaded memory [is] now at last recovered" (C. S. Lewis, *The Screwtape Letters*).

In that moment of connection the questions, frustrations, disappointments, and heartaches of our lives either receive their answer or die away. Then we are able to say with C. S. Lewis's narrator in *Till We Have Faces,* "You are yourself the answer. Before your face, questions die away. What other answer would suffice?"

"I heard a loud shout from the throne, saying, 'Look, the home of God is now among his people! He will live with them, and they will be his people. God himself will be with them. He will remove all of their sorrows, and there will be no more death or sorrow or crying or pain. For the old world and its evils are gone forever'" (Rev. 21:3, 4).

This is but the beginning of the eternal moment of joy.

Because God
Loves You

Three Words

Words are important. A single one can bring to mind a collection of images and memories. The name of a person or place seems to contain something of the essence of that particular individual or location. Similarly, various words carry with them hints of possibilities and glimpses of a deeper meaning.

A few months ago a column in a local newspaper asked for suggestions as to the most significant word in the English language. Readers sent in many interesting suggestions. However, the word the columnist selected was "why."

"**why** *adv.* for what? for what cause, reason, or purpose?" *(Macquarie Concise Dictionary)*.

"Why" deserves its place among the most significant of English words. It is a question in itself—and one of the most important ones we can ask. We learn to use it at a young age. Many parents can attest to the frustration caused by the repeated single-word question in response to every answer—"Why?"

So many things in life require explanations. A recent survey found that "a clear purpose for living" was second only to good health in what people wanted most in life (Barna Research Group). Put simply, we want to know why. Too often, though, we find no easy answers.

However, as we get older—even though we still look for meaning and purpose—we may lose the instinct to ask why: "Why do we
do the things we do? Why do we do them that particular way? Why
do we think the way we do? Why do we feel this way?" But even
if we stop raising these questions, a couple more may continue to
haunt us: "Why do we keep on asking questions, looking for meaning? Or why have we given up asking but still feel there are things
we want to know?"

It may be that we encounter some words and ideas that we cannot fully understand but that capture our imaginations in a way we
can never quite ignore. The words stir in us an ache—a feeling of
absence—and with a mixture of fear and exhilaration we face their
unknown possibilities. "Eternity" is one such word.

"**eternity** *n*. **1.** infinite time; duration without beginning or end.
2. eternal existence, esp. as contrasted with mortal life" *(Macquarie
Concise Dictionary)*.

"Eternity" more firmly embedded itself in the consciousness of
Australia and the world by its inclusion in the fireworks marking
New Year's Eve 1999. Its prominence has sparked new interest in
the story of Sydney's "Mr. Eternity"—Arthur Stace.

Stace grew up in extreme poverty in Sydney in the 1890s. After
serving in World War I, he became a drunk on the streets of Sydney.
However, in 1930 he wandered into a men's meeting at an inner-
city church and became a Christian. About two years later Stace attended a Baptist church in Darlinghurst, where the preacher spoke
on the subject of "eternity."

Inspired by the message, Stace accepted the challenge to spread
"eternity all over the streets of Sydney." Although he could barely
write his own name, he picked up a piece of chalk and wrote the
single word on the footpath in front of the church. It was the beginning of a 35-year commitment.

Although Stace married and worked for a time for the Red
Cross in Sydney, his passion was for this single word—and the im-

pact it could have upon the people of Sydney. The word appeared mysteriously in distinctive, copperplate script across the city for more than 15 years before someone discovered that Arthur Stace was its origin. He continued his adopted work until his death in 1967. It is estimated that he wrote the word "eternity" more than 500,000 times in chalk on the streets of Sydney. On New Year's Eve 1999 his one-word message and the challenge to the reader found a much wider audience as television broadcast Sydney's celebration around the world.

However, it is not just a catchy phrase or clever marketing ploy. The word's significance does not come from the fact of mere repetition. Neither should we embrace it merely because a fireworks display featured it to mark the tick over to 2000. "Eternity" has a resonance. It may well be that—as the Bible suggests—eternity is "planted" in the "human heart" (Eccl. 3:11).

The Bible tells of another word written into the history and hearts of humanity. Referred to simply as "the Word," Scripture says that "the Word became human and lived here on earth among us" (John 1:14). The word has implications of eternity, as Jesus Christ, the eternal God, became human. Truly, "eternity" did become flesh.

However, the Bible employs still another word to refer to the Baby born in Bethlehem almost 2,000 years ago: "Immanuel."

"**Immanuel** *n.* God with us" (see Matt. 1:23).

Early in biblical history God gave His name simply as "I AM" (Ex. 3:14). Significantly, Jesus also used this name to describe Himself (John 8:58, NIV). It was as if God, through Jesus, was saying, "I AM . . . here."

The declaration "Immanuel" was God's answer to many of the questions of the human race. The claims and promises Jesus made have satisfied a lot of the whys from throughout history. He was there at the creation of the world (John 1:3). He lived as a man on this earth in an identifiable place at a particular time in history, experiencing the pains and joys of being a human. He died and was resurrected to open the way to eternity. And He promised that He will come back again to finally end the problems of suffering, death, and pain. The Bible tells us that eternity will answer the whys that still remain unanswered. God gave the first glimpse of His eternal answer in "the Word" made flesh—Jesus Christ.

But until then questions remain. So many things still escape our understanding. We always have more to learn. However, the most important answer we can pursue is a knowledge of God. Each of us needs to get to know Jesus as Immanuel—God with us. When we come face to face with the eternal enormity of God becoming human and dwelling among us, we find ourselves left with one more "Why" question: Why did God do this?

Why? The answer to that requires another three significant but simple words: "God loves you" (see John 3:16).

Does God
Watch Football?

I was doing the tourist thing—and I was rapidly reaching the conclusion that it was crazy!

It was an unpleasant Victorian winter's night, exacerbated for me by my recent descent from the warmer latitudes of Queensland. Nevertheless, we had decided to spend an evening in the outdoors—an eco-tour discovering the nocturnal animals of the Victorian bush. The further discomfort of intermittent showers, dripping trees, and dampness underfoot exacerbated the challenge of the cold.

Our group of adventurers gathered in the gloomy parking lot. We were the hardy few, forgoing the comforts of home and hearth for the challenge and education of picking our way through the darkness in the hope of glimpsing examples of Australia's unique fauna. Just to make the trip on such a night indicated everyone's commitment.

As we handed out flashlights, retrieved raincoats, and made last-minute restroom visits, a woman at the back of the group let out a cry. When the group turned toward her to discover the reason for such an exclamation, we noticed that she held a small radio to her ear. When she realized that we were watching her, she smiled nervously.

"He got the ball," she explained ambiguously and dropped her eyes again, focusing on the radio broadcast.

Her friends came to her rescue: "We had to drag her away from watching football on TV tonight. She's the mother of . . . " They gave a player's name that even I, with my overwhelming ignorance of the Australian Football League, recognized.

In light of this information the anxious mother began to receive renewed respect, particularly by a couple of the males in the group who had more than a passing interest in football.

We made our way into the damp, nocturnal bush, pausing sporadically while the guide pointed out an occasional bedraggled and distant possum or some similar small furry creature. Once we got away from the guide's powerful spotlight, near-total darkness surrounded us. The damp and cold seeped into our clothes and shoes.

The group soon stretched into a ragged line. Yet the hiss of radio static, fragments of football commentary, and the muted comments and cheers of the attentive listener punctuated each stop amid the dripping of cold rain and the otherwise quiet of the bush.

As we trudged through the black night, I was struck by the commitment of this mother to her big, tough, football-playing son in another city, possibly unaware of her dedication to every mention he received in the radio commentary.

I had recently read Umberto Eco's description of the first time he doubted the existence of God and any meaning in life as taking place when, as a teenager, he attended a soccer match. "As I was observing with detachment the senseless movement down there on the field, I felt how the high noonday sun seemed to enfold men and things in a chilling light, and how before my eyes a cosmic, meaningless performance was proceeding."

I wonder if Eco's conclusion may have been different if he had been observing the mother with whom I spent an evening wandering through the Victorian bush.

The Bible asks whether a mother can forget her child or have no compassion for it. The answer is that even though that might happen—and tragically it sometimes does—God will not forget you. The Lord goes so far as to say, "See, I have written your name on my hand" (Isa. 49:16).

So does God watch football? Of course He does. But it is not from a lofty viewpoint, high in the grandstand. The Lord watches football—and everything else you or I do in life—with the intensity of a mother, at the same time cheering and fearing for us. He is saddened by our mistakes, excited by our successes, and sympathetic to our hurts.

Even if that mother forgot her son, God would not forget you. Caring intensely, He loves eternally.

The Sacrifice

The last notes of the singing die away, and the congregation sits. A hush falls across the church as the pastor leads out a sheep. People assume it must be a prop for the children's story. A couple of parents start pushing their small children toward the front of the church. But the pastor does not speak. Usually he welcomes the congregation with a smile and an attempt at a joke, but this morning his face is more solemn than you have ever seen.

He leads the animal to a space in front of the pulpit, where he stops and surveys the crowd. Having taken off his suit coat, he wears just shirt and tie. The grim expression on his face has stilled the congregation, and the church is absolutely silent. Still without speaking, the pastor reaches over the top of the pulpit—and you see he has a large knife.

Haven't you heard something about this kind of thing in the Old Testament? But we don't do that anymore, do we? Somebody said something about sacrificing sheep in Sabbath school last week. What was that about?

"Because of your sins," says the pastor, looking across the audience. The microphone picks up the sound of the sharpening tool he runs along the knife blade. His statement and the metallic grating echo around the sanctuary. The children stand completely still in the aisle.

In a single movement the pastor bends down and cuts the throat

146

of the unresisting sheep. He holds the animal as it begins to struggle and the first drops of blood splatter on the church's spotless carpet and his clean shirt. Picking up a small wooden bowl, he holds the dying sheep in a headlock and catches most of the creature's blood in the bowl. Within a couple of minutes the sheep stops struggling, and its dead body remains where it fell. The pastor begins to move around the front of the church, sprinkling blood on all the items of furniture. He splashes the carefully arranged flowers with the congealing blood of the sheep. His shirtsleeves are also stained with blood.

Imagine how you would feel. The audience would be in a state of shock. A chill of horror would fill the church. The sight of this bloody death would sicken many. Children would have nightmares. There would be tears and anger. It is likely many of the congregation would leave in protest, and some would probably report the pastor to the authorities for cruelty to animals. If the media found the story, there would likely be national coverage, debate, and outrage.

Once, such "worship" was an everyday event. God employs such symbols to give us something visible and tangible that would enable us to begin to grasp His big plan for redeeming humanity. Soon after Adam and Eve's first sin God gave the promise of a Savior (Gen. 3:15), and the most powerful and disturbing symbol of what that Redeemer would be about was the sacrifice of a lamb. To experience such a sacrifice would be a gruesome reminder of how serious a problem sin is in God's eyes, but it also contained the grand truth that our sins are forgiven by an innocent substitute paying sin's penalty for us.

Such sacrifices continued to be an important feature of the relationship between God and His people during the following centuries. In the stories of Noah, Abraham, Isaac, Jacob, and others, building an altar and offering sacrifices were important markers of their journeys and experiences with the Lord.

The building of the sanctuary by the Israelites in the desert was a renewal and expansion of the symbol of sacrifice. However much the idea might repulse us, the sacrifice of animals was a regular and central component of the worship of God throughout the Old

Testament and found a particular focus in the services held at the sanctuary in the desert and later in the Temple in Jerusalem.

Centuries later—when John the Baptist introduced Jesus to the crowds as "the Lamb of God who takes away the sin of the world!" (John 1:29)—we find the one to whom all the generations of sacrifices pointed. The variety of sacrifices detailed in Leviticus had different purposes, and each would be applied to an appropriate occasion, audience, or sin.

But Jesus was *the* sacrifice. In His death He paid the price for all sins—not just for the individual sinner (as detailed in Lev. 4:27), not just for the leader's sins (verse 22), and not just for the sin of the community (verse 13), but for the sin of the whole world, including us.

Jesus is God's sacrifice to erase the sin of the world. The God who has been sinned against loves us so much that He provided the remedy for our sins at great cost to Himself (check out John 3:16 again).

But the sacrifices performed at the sanctuary also remind us of the assurance we can have because of Jesus' sacrifice. When a person recognized their sin and chose to repent, an innocent victim took the penalty in place of the sinner, and the priest took the blood to make atonement for that sin (Lev. 4:27-31). God made a clear promise about those who made such an offering: "they will be forgiven" (verse 31).

Thankfully, we don't need to sacrifice sheep in our church services. Jesus sacrificed Himself for us. When we choose Him, we are forgiven.

The Anti-Art
of Controphy

Controphy—derived from conversational dystrophy—is the name given (by me, as a very amateur sociologist) to the tendency of conversations to degenerate in quality and subject matter. Sometimes they go by huge leaps from the sublime to the ridiculous, other times by gradual and almost imperceptible steps.

Now, it is possible that I am aware of it just because I am usually involved in the conversations that I have greatest opportunity to observe. Certainly, we all know people whose involvement in a conversation soon precipitates a rapid controphic effect, and it may be that I am one of those people unwittingly armed with a barrage of conversation killers. However, when I have had opportunity to discuss this theory with others, I get the impression that it is a widespread phenomenon—but we soon drift into some other topic.

We can observe controphy in every form of social interaction. However, nowhere does it manifest itself more dramatically than in the discussion of matters of Christianity and religion. The potential difference between the height and breadth of the mind of God and the mundane pettiness of religious trappings provides a vast scope in which the controphy inherent in all discussions can run rampant. The significance of the topic exaggerates the enormity of the decline.

Consider the standard controphic pattern. Occasionally a discussion, whether it be in a Bible study group or in a less-formal conversation, can approach a subject matter dealing with the awesomeness of God. Yet within a few minutes the group will be debating—usually with increasing vigor—the appropriateness or otherwise of swimming on Sabbath afternoon or some similar "standard." Controphy has done its work, a pattern repeated many times over. It almost seems that the degree of controphy is proportional to the magnitude of the subject initially under discussion.

It is hardly surprising, then, that discussion of the grace of God is especially prone to this degenerative condition. As the grandest of all themes available for study and discussion, it is worthy of much more careful attention. However, as soon as grace gets preached, discussed, or even mentioned, someone quickly wants to point out "the other side of grace," and the conversation descends into an articulation of appropriate behaviors.

Yet there is no "other side" to grace. If you are looking for some requirement for the party to whom the grace has been given, it ceases to be grace, becoming a mere exchange of behavior and reward. In all honesty, when we stand at the cross, what do we have that we can legitimately exchange for the boundless love of the God of the universe? If we do have to offer something, then we are just as hopelessly lost as when we began. As soon as any mention of something in addition to the simple but unfathomable grace of God is made, the discussion has entered into an alarming and dangerous controphy.

It is so much simpler and a real temptation to talk about Christian behavior and standards—or the weather or sports results, for that matter. Perhaps that is why Paul opens all his letters by acknowledging God's grace, thus continually bringing his readers back to it, and he closes his letters as well by returning to God's grace and commending it to their recipients. It may also be that he knew from personal experience the power and overwhelming importance of grace: "But whatever I am now, it is all because God poured out his special favor on me" (1 Cor. 15:10). Could we gain a fuller appreciation of God's grace, our spiritual conversations may not be so controphic.

Controphy can be frustrating, but it can also be a way of escaping topics of conversation that make us feel uncomfortable. God forbid that His amazing grace should be one of them. Yet, however we approach it and however our conversations might degenerate, the grace itself remains unchanged. That is its very nature.

In the grand conversation that is God's communication with humanity both generally and individually, there is no controphy. Instead, we find the unshakable assurance that God's grace remains and is always available to us no matter what our past failures or present circumstance. The grace of God depends only upon the unfailing goodness of God Himself.

The Gentle Art of Tipping

I n Australian parlance, tipping usually has more to do with which horse or football team will win on a weekend. Yet tipping—giving a small amount of money above the standard charge in appreciation of a service rendered—is a subtle art, with various shades of generosity of spirit accompanying the gift.

A few years ago I took up the red vinyl warming box and joined the forces of Australia's pizza delivery drivers. There are not too many jobs available to someone beyond the age of 18 and thus no longer eligible for junior wages; who has too many qualifications but who is not able to commit to working 30-something or more hours per week; and who does not want to work on weekends. Yes, it is quite possible that I should have had higher ethical standards and not surrendered so easily to the ranks of corporate lackey and purveyor of junk food to the already overweight masses. Yet in the course of my employment during those few months I had ample opportunity to appreciate the finer points of the art of tipping.

Of course, the most common example is the nontip—and there is nothing necessarily wrong with this. The purchaser exchanges the price for the product, satisfactorily concluding the transaction. The next most common tip is that of giving change to the nearest dollar, usually leaving between 5 and 15 cents as a small bonus. It is similar to the next form, the larger "keep the change" amounts. The inherent ambiguity of such tips leaves the recipient unsure as to whether the tip is the result of laziness, impatience, or generosity.

By far, the nicest tips are those that are obviously intentional. They not only have correct change but an additional amount added. It is a simple act of kindness—an act of grace—that brightens an evening, not to mention helping to pay for car fuel.

However, the kind of tipping that would truly astound any pizza deliverer would be that of the completely random and unscheduled tip. And it is healthier, too: no pizza involved. It would be someone simply stopping you in the street and giving you something, perhaps so unexpectedly that it might even offend you. Such things just do not make sense.

Yet God seems to be into this type of tipping. Individually and as a planet we were wandering along the street of life—going nowhere in particular—only to be interrupted by the most unexpected tip in the universe. We were not delivering anything to God—we had nothing to give. "But God showed his great love for us by sending Christ to die for us while we were still sinners" (Rom. 5:8).

And to take this irrational tipping a huge step further, consider that the tip might not be just enough to help you buy some gas that day. Instead, it is enough to buy you a new car—in fact, it means you never have to work again. You are set for life. By this stage you would be calling into question the sanity of such a tipper.

This is grace: "I know very well how foolish the message of the cross sounds to those who are on the road to destruction. But we who are being saved recognize this message as the very power of God" (1 Cor. 1:18). In Christ God gave you the craziest, most extravagant tip in the history of the universe.

Grace does not make any sense, but we should be overwhelmingly grateful that it doesn't. If God dealt with us with mere justice, we would find ourselves quickly back on our dead-end street—going nowhere in particular. The nonsense of grace is our only hope.

By a strange but truly divine logic, the inexplicable grace of God has become the strongest force in the universe—the biggest, craziest tipping ever seen. "This 'foolish' plan of God is far wiser than the wisest of human plans, and God's weakness is far stronger than the greatest of human strength" (verse 25).

The Greatest
Art: Grace

Dorothy Sayers suggests that we
should view God as an artist who
"does not see life as a problem to be solved,
but as a medium for creation" (as quoted by
Philip Yancey). However, unlike an artist
who steps back to get a proper look at the work in progress, God put
Himself into the picture Himself. In Jesus the Artist became a part of
the art so as to be able to complete His work more effectively.

Grace is not just a nice thought or a good idea. It became—and
continues to be—a Person and an action. The process whereby He
creates is grace. In the great work of art that is life grace is the tools,
the medium, and the work of art itself.

Yet it is still a work-in-progress. Put simply, you are a bad person in a bad place. The more theologically correct statement of your
condition would be that you are a sinner in a fallen world. The only
way your situation could be worse is if you were a sinner in a fallen
world without a Savior. Left to ourselves, we will die and our world
self-destruct. According to C. S. Lewis the death of Christ was necessary precisely because men are not worth dying for.

Thankfully, though, that is not the end of the story. Grace is the
glorious and abundant certainty that gives us hope. Not the prodigal
son's father reluctantly forgiving his repentant son when he finally got
enough sense to come back home and, kneeling in the dust, to plead
for forgiveness, it is rather the Father's love and forgiveness reaching

out to the son while he was still in the far country before he even had any thought of a return home (Luke 15). Of course, the son had yet to accept the Father's grace, but this by no means diminished its power.

In describing his own grudging acceptance of the truth of Christianity, C. S. Lewis marvels at the humility found in God's grace—that He would continue to extend grace to a person so unwilling. "The Prodigal Son at least walked home on his own feet. But who can duly adore that Love which will open the high gates to a prodigal who is brought in kicking, struggling, resentful, and darting his eyes in every direction for a chance of escape?" Again, Lewis sees the Lord working in an unexpected and irrational but altogether glorious manner: "The hardness of God is kinder than the softness of men, and His compulsion is our liberation."

In the context of Paul's personal experience of God's grace, the apostle expresses a similar wonder: "We praise God for the wonderful kindness he has poured out on us because we belong to his dearly loved Son. He is so rich in kindness that he purchased our freedom through the blood of his Son, and our sins are forgiven. He has showered his kindness on us, along with all wisdom and understanding" (Eph. 1:6-8).

Grace finds beauty in everything and makes even more beauty out of what are otherwise ugly things. As the master Artist, God creates beauty in us, His people and recipients of His grace. "God saved you by his special favor when you believed. And you can't take credit for this; it is a gift from God. Salvation is not a reward for the good things we have done, so none of us can boast about it. For we are God's masterpiece. He has created us anew in Christ Jesus, so that we can do the good things he planned for us long ago" (Eph. 2:8-10).

As a carefully crafted artwork of grace, we can be assured that we are of immense personal value to Him. But His grace working in us adds to His glory—not to ours. The joyous truth is that no matter who we are, wherever we are, whatever our past or present circumstances might be, God loves us—unconditionally and unquestionably, infinitely and eternally. This is the simple but transcendent grace: God loves you.

The Beginning

I t's one of the all-time great closing scenes. The hero has made his dramatic speech, the heroine has made her heart-rending choice, and her plane climbs into the sky from Casablanca, leaving Rick (played by Humphrey Bogart) with his memories. But the 1942 classic *Casablanca* has one final moment—an improbable friendship between two rivals forged by the absurdity of their circumstances.

As the sound of the plane dies away, the camera draws back on Rick and the French police officer disappearing into the foggy night. Just before the credit music swells, Rick drawls to his companion, "Louis, I think this is the beginning of a beautiful friendship."

It is an unlikely alliance—but friendships are the strangest things, often defying logical explanation. Circumstances draw us together, and common interests and shared experiences help us grow closer. Such relationships are perhaps the most undefinable, inexplicable, and yet most profound facets of our lives. True friendship cannot be created artificially—but it is created.

When God brought our world into being, He personally spent time with Adam and Eve, walking with them in the Garden of Eden. When the first couple sinned, this close relationship was no longer possible—in fact, they hid from God when they heard Him walking in search of them (Gen. 3:8).

But the Creator already had a plan to rebuild that relationship. He first worked through the people of Israel and lived among them, starting in the sanctuary tent and then in the Temple built in Jerusalem. However, His plan found its fullest reality in Jesus, who was God once again walking with people on the streets of our world. He was "God with us" (Matt. 1:23).

In His dying for us Jesus paid the price and made the way for our permanent reconnection with God. He promised to send the Holy Spirit to live in us as a continuing divine presence, and He vowed that that connection will one day be fully restored as once again we can live in the actual presence of God (Rev. 21:3). It's an incredible promise.

The Bible uses so many different ways to represent God to us. Some of them can be frightening. Others are more comforting, such as the images of a loving father or mother. All of them are important and help us have a balanced picture of Him and His love. But perhaps the most appealing is that of God simply being with us. Throughout the Bible He repeatedly asks His people for a place and time He can share with them. The language God uses suggests some of the simplest forms of personal interaction: wanting simply to hang out with us, to go for a hike (or a more gentle stroll, if you prefer), to have a meal together and to talk—sometimes seriously, sometimes more lightheartedly. And, ultimately, to live with us forever.

The bottom line is friendship. Wouldn't it be incredible to be such friends with God that just for a moment—one day—you simply forgot it was God (not in a careless or sacrilegious way) with whom you were friends—that He was simply your friend? He gives us the invitation to begin this adventure today and start growing that incredible friendship that will last forever.

God created us to connect with Him, to be His friends, and to spend time with Him as part of His family. Indeed, we find our true purpose in a close relationship with Him, but, as we live our everyday lives, that relationship has an unfinished element to it. As yet, we receive only glimpses of what that friendship might be. We can take positive steps to spend time with God and get to know Him now. And we have the promise that He will be with us—He will walk beside us in our lives—every step of the way (Matt. 28:20). It is an awesome and present privilege. This is the beginning of a beautiful—and eternal—friendship.

"But for right now, until that completeness, we have three things to do to lead us toward that consummation: Trust steadily in God, hope unswervingly, love extravagantly" (1 Cor. 13:13, Message).